A MANUAL

of

Style and Standards
in Academic Writing, Editing
and Publishing

A MANUAL

of

Style and Standards in Academic Writing, Editing and Publishing

With Some Thoughts on Research, Education and Training in Publishing // Context: Bangladesh, South Asia and Similar Non-English Speaking Regions

Professor Manzurul Islam, PhD

Partridge Singapore

PARTRIDGE
A Penguin Random House Company

Library of Congress Control Number: 2015958736
ISBN: Softcover   978-1-4828-5440-4
              eBook   978-1-4828-5439-8

In collaboration with The Scholar, the publishing wing of The Centre for
Development through Open Learning, Publishing and Communication
(CEDOLPC). Building 9, 'Mandevilla', Suite A-3, Road 14, Sector 1,
Uttara Model Town, Dhaka 1230, Bangladesh.

Print information available on the last page.

To order additional copies of this book, contact
Toll Free 800 101 2657 (Singapore)
Toll Free 1 800 81 7340 (Malaysia)
orders.singapore@partridgepublishing.com

www.partridgepublishing.com/singapore

Dedicated to the young academics, researchers,
graduate students, Authors and Editors
of publications in English
who may not have ready access
to handy, quick consultation facility
from the various sources,
but who wish to maintain acceptable standards
in presentation of their painstaking writings.

Table of Contents (in short)

Foreword

by Chairman,
University Grants Commission of Bangladesh

I have the pleasure to introduce this Manual of Style and Standards for the authors, editors and academics of universities and research organizations, specially in the context of Bangladesh, South Asia and similar non-English speaking countries. Any university or organization that wishes to undertake academic and research publications also as one of its primary responsibilities, will find this a useful and handy guidebook.

Our universities and research organizations have been publishing books, journals and other materials following various practices. Since there was no proper single-volume source of guidebook or style manual, we had to rely on several sources, thus often making room for unintentional inconsistencies and other lapses.

As every university wishes to advance with quality, along with its expansion programs in all directions, an important sector like publications cannot be neglected for long. A handy Guidebook or Style Manual has been a long-felt need in this respect. This will now be made easier for the potential authors, young teachers and researchers, in matters of consistency and house style. It is to this end that we believe that publication of one such Manual, containing suitable contents specially for academic, scientific and research publications in English -- the common language of our journals and other publications in the international context, will play a significant role. Dissemination of knowledge and scholarship through the print media shall continue side by side with other modern technology-based media.

I congratulate the present compiler-author, Professor Dr Manzurul Islam, an international expert in his field, for his pioneering venture; he has worked abroad in universities and research organizations for twenty-seven years and in Bangladesh for over two decades.

Part Two of the book contains valuable discussion and recommendations for education and training of editors and publishing professionals; this also signifies the great role of standard writing and editing in furthering research and publication – a task all universities and institutions of higher learning must fulfill.

I would urge all academic writers, researchers, editors and practitioners to provide the compiler-author with more feedback so that after proper review, some of those could be considered for incorporation into the next edition. As an academician and now an educational administrator of the country, I would like to thank Professor Manzur once again for this unique and timely work.

I very much hope this modest but very significant work will prove as a remarkable contribution.
I wish the concise Manual of Style and Standards for publications in English a great success with a wide readership and followers.

Professor Abdul Mannan
October 2015.

Introduction
by the Author

**A Manual of Style and Standards and Role of Publishing,
specially in the context of universities and research
organizations in Bangladesh, South Asia and similar other
non-English speaking regions**

PART ONE

It has been long felt that a Style Manual be prepared for the
Authors, Academics and Researchers of universities and research
organizations as well as for their Editors, Copyeditors and technical
personnel. This would help them adopt consistency, house style
and an acceptable standard.

Some universities follow in general The Chicago Manual of Style
and MLA Handbook or APA Guide or Harvard Style Guides
or specific manuals for respective disciplines. Some institutions
introduce their own style mostly based on procedures followed in
reputed universities and establishments or in places where their
senior authors and editors have had their education and training.
This resulted in various practices and incoherent procedures in the
same organization or in the same group of publications.

Procedures and standard practices are compiled, sometimes re-written, and presented in the current Manual for adoption of a consistent style. Options or alternative practices are provided for the users or their authorities to decide a single one for themselves. These are based on varied experiences of the Faculty, Authors, Editors and technical staff involved in the process of writing, editing and publishing.

For details of regular rules and common linguistic practices in English, authors and practitioners may turn to a recent edition of any standard book on English grammar, usage and style. They may also consult various reference books. Some such well-consulted books are listed at the end of this Manual. All Authors, Teachers and Learners should avoid unauthenticated or pirated reference books and dictionaries cheaply available in the market; such sub-standard publications will mislead and confuse readers, users and hardworking scholars and authors.

For our Authors and Editors, the present Manual outlines some basic concepts and practices and presents common rules or procedures. Some are suggested for consideration of further review and study and then for implementation. A few are slightly deviated from the international standards, to make room for acceptable local context, based on research and study.

Some notes and brief description on a few related topics like plagiarism, rights, intellectual property, permission, e-journals, self-publishing, editors' ethics, etc. are included for the benefit of new Authors.

One must realize, in the context of non-English speaking countries, English is at best a second language to most of our Authors and Editors of today, a large number of whom had to pursue their early education and undergraduate studies through the medium of national or regional language. Nevertheless, the Authors must attempt to follow as much international standard as possible. Unconventional styles may also be acceptable only after expert review if some special or uncommon practices are adopted for the convenience of local Authors and Editors as well as for a comfortable continuity.

Editors as the last check-post for Authors, specially here in non-English speaking countries, cannot be much too rigid for full perfection. To encourage more and more authorship, and to publish as early as possible materials of otherwise significant research and value, with minimum complications both at the Editor's and the Author's ends, some flexibility should be allowed to all concerned. On the contrary, to maintain quality and international standard, efforts should always be made to attain maximum credibility. In all cases, consistency and correctness should be valued much. Such a careful, double-pronged approach by Authors and Editors alike, with due role by each, would benefit all concerned. This will also serve the production and editing quality in an ever growing creative and professional publishing industry in the developing regions.

As part of Quality Assurance programs by the better placed universities, it is heartening to observe that some of these institutions of higher education and research have been recently making progressive attempts to modernize, popularize and expand the profession of scientific and academic publishing for higher or tertiary level education. Some have taken into serious consideration, and rightly so, the 'publish or perish' concept. Already in recent years, quite a few universities, both public and private, have brought out some publications in superior quality. And this too at times has been with the strength of a comparatively small size of faculty or professional staff who genuinely care for quality.

As an example, one study showed that in some particular years, more than 150 scientific and research journals were published in Bangladesh; many of these are often irregular in frequency and also leave much scope for improvement in content, editing and production quality. Of the problems in content, organization, language, presentation and readability, use of English language was found to be a vital area for special attention. [The present compiler-author experienced this during his forty-five years or more of first-hand working with publications in several non-English speaking countries like Bangladesh, Pakistan, India, Malaysia, Singapore, Saudi Arabia, Egypt, etc]. This is assumed as natural in the socio-political context of each such country.

Qualified language editors in such places could play a significant role and could contribute more towards further improvement in quality learned publishing. This is because, better or more perfect use of English by most of our junior and new authors cannot be expected in today's context, when national or regional languages are given more importance, and rightly so. As models or guides, our seasoned and senior Authors may not be in a mood or need to write and publish more, after they attained permanent and desired tenure, professorship, or senior age. It is mostly the young or less experienced Authors whom we should support and encourage to publish more and more and in maximum possible quality. Editors and mentors have to come forward to be by the side of new Authors, specially when it relates to writing and editing in English. This is considered an important aspect to produce and publish more and to see a larger size of successful authorship. The same applies also to the increasing number of today's corporate bodies who have often to deal with publications in various forms – books, reports, official or promotion literature, etc. They have to keep in mind that nothing in print should go unedited, or without proper copyediting and proofreading, preferably by professional linguists or Editors or closely associated qualified personnel.

The number of scholarly and scientific publications by our universities must have to be on the increase if our institutions are to be recognized globally and if the quality of scholarship and knowledge by the Faculty has to be upheld. In fact all Schools and Departments of our universities in particular should give priority to this aspect -- publishing standard works in addition to preparing and publishing credible textbooks with minimum technical flaws.

While users would do well to follow this Manual to the maximum extent, they may turn to other standard works and to their own experienced judgment for further details and decisions. The Compiler-author of this concise Manual wishes to acknowledge with gratitude all authors and organizations of standard books or guides on Style, specially those by the universities of Oxford, Cambridge, Stanford, Harvard, Minnesota, British Columbia and a few others that were readily available at his desk. These were consulted freely. Thanks are also due to the colleagues and young 'teacher trainees' in the various Workshops conducted from time to time by the present Author in different universities; they supported the work all through and pursued the Compiler to prepare a book. I am grateful to my other colleagues from both developing and advanced regions – specially in the places I worked over the years – who shared views with me, not necessarily always agreeing.

This small work, enriched from scanned, voluminous worksheets and notes, must grow as time passes, subsequently leading to the compilation of a full-fledged comprehensive guidebook. Our academics and authors can well recollect that the much-consulted Chicago Manual of Style started as an in-house Manual in 1906, only in a few pages first; then it grew into the current voluminous work of 1026 pages, running into its 16th edition in 2010.

My sincere apologies for the shortcomings which are my own and which would be expected to be addressed by me or by my successors in the next edition(s).

PART TWO

Considering some relevance to academic and research writing, editing and publishing in the context of Bangladesh and other non-English speaking regions, a few Articles and Notes on training and education in Publishing, university presses, and scholarly publishing are supplemented. Most of these are adapted, with minor changes, from a few of the many such Articles and Papers by the Author and published or presented elsewhere. Sincere thanks are due to the Publishers or sponsors of such journals, conferences, and publications that brought out those first.

Research and publication, together with pedagogy, have always played a significant role in faculty development in the universities and colleges of the country. This small book is expected to inspire and assist young academics and researchers to concentrate on their skill development in publication, through better acquaintance with the various procedures and practices of writing and editing in particular. These in themselves will also contribute to quality assurance measures in any university or research organization. Today's internet or online facilities have opened up effective avenues to consult promptly relevant materials, but again to present something handy and in print, to be by the side of every new or would-be Author, Researcher or Editor, the current compilation should be of some service.

The second part of the book also covers some thoughts by an academic and professional in respect of many of the topics presented in the first part.

In countries like Bangladesh and other non-English speaking regions, publishing has special challenges to address. In addition to some form of special usage of language and style, some major and reputed Publishers and Authors follow occasionally typical practices. These again are considered as models for less experienced Authors and local Publishers. From time to time and from Publisher to Publisher, these keep on changing, often showing signs of improvement and eagerness for adaptation in the light of contemporary usage and local context. Examples of these are presented in different sections of *the Manual*.

Some excerpts from a number of recent Workshops designed and directed by the Author of this Manual, and conducted by senior academics and specialists from various disciplines, are appended in the current volume. For the practice of consistency in style, guidelines are provided.

While reviewing practices and style in this *Manual,* the target users have been assumed to be:
Authors and Editors; Young Scholars, Academics and Researchers; Graduate Students preparing for Masters and PhD Theses and Dissertations; Librarians, Personnel in the Information Services and Publication Departments and also the common practitioners in writing, editing and publishing.

Original plan to publish the book in February (since then delayed by over six months) was a bit coincidental; the month in Bangladesh has turned out to be the month of new publications, apart from its being a very glorious time of the year in honor of mother language. This year, over four thousand new titles have been exhibited which is more than the total number of publications during any full year. However, as is normal, a small percentage of this belongs to academic and research publishing. This last segment must grow rapidly and in standard quality, if our knowledge industry has to survive in the print media and if capacity building of our young Teachers in the academia also through publication works has any relevance. To that end too, the present *Manual* is expected to be helpful.

Manzurul Islam
Center for Development through Open Learning, Publishing and Communication
(CEDOLPC), Dhaka
12 October 2015

PART ONE (Contents in detail)

Chapter 1

LANGUAGE AND STYLE

[GENERAL NOTE: Examples are provided in smaller font, 10 point roman light, immediately following the description in the text which is in larger font, in 12 point roman.]

1.1 SPELLING

1.1.1 American Spelling.

a) Particularly, the ending –ize and –ization is preferred to – ise and –isation in words where this alternative exists.

Example:

civilize, civilization
minimize, minimization
organize, organization
specialize, specialization

b) Some words should be spelt with an 's'.

Example:

Advertise   paralyse   supervise

c) Other common words include:

Example:

> program (in place of programme)
> color (in place of colour)
> advisor (in place of adviser)
> honor (in place of honour)
> favor (in place of favour)
> encyclopedia (in place of encyclopaedia)

d) A few nouns that end in re / er

Example:

center	fiber	meter	theater
(centre)	(fibre)	(metre)	(theatre)

NOTE: With the common use of computer these days, where mostly auto-spell checker is available, details are avoided here. Only a few are described.

1.1.2 Some Common Misspelled Words

accommodate   all right   argument   awkward

census	chlorophyll	comparative	consensus	
consistency	correspondence	develop	diarrhea	dysentery
embarrass	exaggerate	except	excerpt	
fulfillment				
grammar				

harass   hemorrhage   honorary   hypothesis
insistence   independence
liaison   labeled

millennium   misspell
necessarily

occasional   occurrence
ophthalmology
parallel

privilege
preferred
pronunciation

recommendation
resistance
rhythm
separate

tendency
transfer
thorough

until

1.1.3 Some Confusing Similar-Sounding and Similarly Spelled Words, Having Different Meanings

accept (take)	except (omit)
advice (noun)	advise (verb)
affect (influence)	effect (result, impact)
all ready (prepared)	already (previously)
altogether (completely)	all together (in total)
ascent (climb)	assent (agreement)
bloc (group of persons or companies)	block (group of things; solid piece)
born (of birth)	borne (carried)
capital (city; significant)	capitol (building)
calendar (list of dates)	calender (a machine for smoothening)
complement (complete)	compliment (praise)
councilor (member of a council)	counsellor (adviser)
dying (coloring)	dying (about to die)
foreword (preface)	forward (ahead)
ordinance (law)	ordnance (weapons)
personal (private)	personnel (staff)
precede (happen before)	proceed (continue)
principal (head)	principle (rule)
stationary (motionless)	stationery (writing materials)
thorough (fully)	through (via)
waive (forego)	wave (move up and down)

1.1.4   Plural Forms of some Nouns

alumnus	alumni
analysis	analyses
appendix	appendixes or appendices
crisis	crises
criterion	criteria
formula	formulae or formulas
index	indexes (of a book) or indices (in mathematics)
matrix	matrices
medium	mediums or media
memorandum	memorandums or memoranda
millennium	millennia or millenniums
nucleus	nuclei
phenomenon	phenomena
symposium	symposiums or symposia

1.2 CAPITALIZATION: General and Special Terminologies

1.2.1   General

[Only a few that are common in scientific and academic journals and books are described. For details, any standard dictionary or grammar may be consulted.]

a) The first letter of each word in a main heading.
    [Formatting: This heading is centered; a style is also in practice for placement of the heading left indented or in the left margin if it appears in an even page or right indented or in the right margin if it is in an odd page].

b) The first word in an outline heading or in a sub-heading is capitalized.

c) The first words of run-in enumerations that form complete sentences are capitalized.

d) The first words of vertical lists and enumerations are capitalized.

However, enumerations of words or phrase run in with the introductory text are generally lowercased.

1.2.2 Computer and IT terms

a) The following are some usages related to the computer and information technology applications, concerning capitalization.

Example:

the Internet (but internet), (the) Net
CD-ROM
World Wide Web or www or (the) Web
Web site or Web pages
iMac
iPod
iPad
PageMaker
QuarkXPress
Adobe Illustrator
Amazon.com

b) Some terms avoid use of capital letters

Example:

e-mail
online
bandwidth
domain

c) It is usual with some industries to use capital letters within the name of a product. As per manufacturer's choice, names of such terms and products are capitalized.

Example:

BASIC   Pascal   COBOL   WordPerfect

1.2.3   Scientific Terms

a) Botanical / Biological terms

New Latin genus names in botany and zoology are capitalized. Scientific name of a phylum, order, class, family is capitalized. The second term in binomial scientific names, identifying the species or subspecies, is lowercased.

Example:

Fusarium flocciferum   Calotropis procera
Commiphora quadricincta   C. quadricincta

(The first word in each of the two names denotes genus while the second word denotes species)

> Arthropoda (phylum)
> Roslaes (order)

b) Chemical and physical terms

  b.1) Spelled-out names of chemical elements and compounds are not capitalized. Capital letters but no periods are used for symbols.

aluminium	Al
zinc	Zn
hydrochloric acid	Hcl

  b.2) Names of laws, theorems, or principles are not capitalized except for proper nouns that are part of the law.

> Ohm's law
> Pythagoras' theorem
> theory of relativity

  b.3) Names of conditions, syndromes and the like are not capitalized. A personal name that forms part of such a term is capitalized.

  Example:

diabetes mellitus	Down syndrome	Parkinson's disease

  b.4) Generic names of drugs are not capitalized.

b.5) Trade names of drugs and manufactured products are capitalized.

Example:

Tylenol   Valium

b.6) Such names are not capitalized when they are established as common nouns.

Example:

styrofoam   nylon

c) Geological terms

c.1) Names of eras, periods, and epochs are capitalized.

c.2) The words era, period, etc. are not capitalized.

Example:

Minjur sandstone
Arabian shield
early Jurassic
Cenzoic era

c.3) When modifiers like early, middle, or late, are used merely for description, these are not capitalized.

Example:

late Jurassic
early Cenzoic

d) Medical and pharmacological terms

d.1) Names of conditions, syndromes and the like are not capitalized. A personal name, which forms part of such a term is capitalized.

Example:

diabetes insipidus
Down syndrome
Parkinson's disease

d.2) Generic names of drugs are not capitalized.

Example:

sulfasalazine
meprobamate
vitamin C

d.3) When a single letter is used as a word, hyphenated or not, it is capitalized.

Example:

X-ray
vitamin D

1.2.4   Special use of Capital Letters in some Places

NOTE: Special for publications by academic and research organizations in Bangladesh and non-English speaking regions

a) Use of capital letters is one of several devices to lend importance or expression or emphasis to certain words in the context of non-English speaking areas. Often such use is avoided in the Western and English speaking countries.

b) It may be noted that the rules provided here are some hints for deciding the use of capital letter. Some of these may be replaced by new rules, even if they clash with the ones illustrated here, depending on the house style or guide followed by a particular institution or publishing organization.

c) To make it distinct and quickly identifiable, the following are capitalized:

c.1) The words Table and Figure are capitalized when these are used for specific tables and figures in the text or in the tables and figures. These are lowercased when used generally.

Example:

The results of the recent survey are summarized in Table 3 and Figure 2.

Some examples should be supported by tables and figures.

c.2) When exclusive references are made to or discussed about some nouns, such words may be capitalized, to stress on these subjects.

Example:

The Author had all the freedom to accept or reject the Reviewer's comments.

The Publisher wanted to offer a Royalty of only 10 %, whereas 12.5% was common at the time.

d) Almost all proper nouns (particular places, persons, names of firms, corporations, and organizations and their members) are capitalized. The list may be too large and hence out of scope here. Any dictionary or other reference material may be consulted.

Example:

Cambridge, Dhaka, Kuala Lumpur; A K Fazlul Huq, Mahatma Gandhi, Winston Churchill; Standard Chartered Bank, Film Development Corporation, Institute of Development Studies, etc.

e) Words such as group, division, department, office, or agency that refer to a specific corporate and organizational unit are capitalized.

Example:

Publishing, Printing and Distribution Division
Training and Research Wing of Administration Division
Training, International Affairs, Research and Publication Division

Bangladesh Biman
Air India
Pakistan International Airlines

School of Education, Bangladesh Open University
Academic Publishing Department, King Saud University
Department of English, Dhaka University.

f) But when this designates no specific names, or departments, it is lower cased.

Example:

All departments of a university belong to some schools or faculties.
A new labor party was introduced in the large meeting last week.

1.2.5   Degrees, Diplomas, Certificates, etc

Example:

Masters in Publishing Science, or MA in English, or Master of Communications
He has been conferred the degree of Masters in Chemistry
He obtained MA in History
He holds a Master of Science degree from Cambridge University
He is a Master of Business Administration
He obtained a postgraduate Diploma in Journalism
He was awarded a Certificate in Spoken English

1.2.6   Seasons, months, days

Example:

Basanta, Boishakh, Aswin
Eid-ul-Fitr, Christmas, Purnima

July, September, December
Friday, Sunday, Tuesday

1.2.7   Religious names and terms

   a)   Names of religious bodies and their members, and derived adjectives are capitalized.

Example:

> Allah, The Quran, The Prophet (but all prophets), The Hadith, Sunnah, The Bible, The Gita, The Tripitak
> Vedas
> Buddhist
> Christian
> Hindu
> Islam
> Muslim
> Shiai'te
> Roman Catholic
> Greek Orthodox

   b)   Words used in a non-religious sense are not capitalized.

Example:

> paradise   heaven   hell   devil   angel   nirvana

   c)   But when we refer to words used in religious sense, they are capitalized.

Example:

> Which Muslim does not wish to be in Paradise?
> Buddhists seek to attain Nirvana.
> God is in Heaven.

d) In run of text, names of some rites and services are not capitalized.

Example:

morning prayer (but Fazr)	evening prayer (but Maghreb)	kuhtbah
mezuzah	sanctuary	rosary

e) Anglicized versions of scientific names are not capitalized.

Example:

primate (from the order Primata)
sequoia (from the genus Sequoia)

f) When referring to specific vitamins, only the letter representing the vitamin is capitalized.

Example:

vitamin C (not Vitamin C)
vitamin B-12/vitamin B_{12}

g) Names of diseases, syndromes, tests, and other medical terms except for proper nouns that are part of the names, are not capitalized.

Example:

malaria
Down's syndrome

1.2.8   The salutation and complimentary close

a)   In the salutation of a letter, capital is used for the first word and all nouns.

Example:

Dear Doctor
Dear Sir
My dear Professor

b)   In a close, only the first word is capitalized, not the others that follow.

Example:

Yours sincerely
Very sincerely yours
Affectionately yours

1.3 USES OF MEASURE, NUMBERS, TIME

1.3.1   Units of measure

a)   Except in tables or technical work, all units of measure are to be spelled out.

b)   Abbreviations for units of measure are identical in the singular and the plural. Periods are not to be used with the symbols of metric units. Spelled-out units are not abbreviated and plurals can be used.

Example:

> 6 ft.   10 ft.   5 kg   30 cm
> 10 kg, but 10 kilograms

1.3.2   Use of numbers, enumeration

1. If a number contains four or more digits, a comma is used between groups of three digits counting from the right.

> 2,305
> 1,564,988

2. Exceptions to the above are: serial numbers, common and decimal fractions, astronomical time, page numbers, addresses, zip code and year numbers.

> Serial number 32697
> .07863
> Cash memo number 00127821
> page 1026
> Gazipur 1705
> 2011

3. Digits (not words) are always used with abbreviations or symbols. Note that periods or dots are not used in the last two:

> 3 hr.   5 lb.   2 in.   5 mm   5 kg

4. Digits are used with the unit of measure when spelling out or abbreviating.

Example:

> 80 kilometers   6 month old   10 lbs   5 cm

5. A unit of measure is abbreviated only with a number.

   Example:

   > The books were weighed in kilograms.
   > The total weight was 90 kg.

6. Days, weeks, years, etc. are treated as units of measure. Digits are used for them.

   Example:

   > The President will visit the region again in 12 months.
   > The Bank will function 6 days a week during the month of Ramadhan.

7. Usually inclusive numbers are used in a running text or in outline form.

   Example:

   > The decade of 2001 – 2010 (instead of 2001 – 10) was full of turmoil.
   > For relevant analysis, look up pages 135 – 139 (instead of 135 – 39).

8. For convenience of easy reading, a comma is used after every group of three digits, starting from the right-hand group. Dates are excepted.

   5, 326   21,332   4,675,332

9. In some countries (specially in continental Europe), commas are avoided and space is used instead.

   Example:

   > 5 326   21 332   4 675 332

10. Ordinal number are most often spelled out.

Example:

Do not commit the same mistake the second time.
He visited an eleventh-century site last year.

Enumeration:

a) Enumerating letter or number is not separated from the beginning of what it follows.

It is carried over to the next line when such an enumerating letter or number takes place at the end of the line.

Example:

When reviewing agricultural development, three issues were considered: (a) weather, (b) technology, and (c) skilled labor.

b) When enumerations run into the text, they are indicated by numerals in parenthesis. These may also be indicated by italic letters. Commas or semicolons are used for separation.

Example:

In the opinion of the Board, strict measures against neglecting personnel will include: (1) Suspension from job, (2) transfer to another department having direct supervision, and (3) termination from employment.

Another way of distinguishing notes added by an editor or translator from those of the author is to use (a) symbols from the former and (b) numbers for the latter.

c) Outline style is followed in case of long enumerations. Here each item begins on a line by itself. Each item will begin with a capital letter and will not use punctuation at the end.

Example:

Among many recommendations, the following appeared acceptable to most participants:

1. Formal education in publishing is needed
2. For such education, some universities should introduce both undergraduate and graduate courses
3. In addition, regular training programs are to be organized from time to time
4. Internship arrangements are to be initiated by large publishing houses
5. Fellowships are to be awarded for distinguished publishing professionals

Figures: Numbers are spelt out in words in the case of purely descriptive matter. Examples: 'Some important revolutions took place in the nineteenth century', 'Living for hundred years is not common', 'only a few universities were established a thousand years ago'.

Numbers under 10 are printed in words, but figures above this are described in numerals. Examples: Eight, Nine, 25, 103, 2015. But in the beginning of a sentence or statement, figures are expressed in words: 'Sixty', not '60'. But '60 to 100', not 'Sixty to 100.'

Numerals are used in statistical matter and Tables.

Numbering in Sections and Sub-sections: Chapters, Paragraphs, Sections, Sub-sections follow these common standards: Relative importance is given when chapters and paragraphs are subdivided into titled or numbered sections or sub-sections. Types and fonts are distinguished from sections to sub-sections. Similarly, spacing between sections or sub-sections and text is followed as per importance, and for variation in layout. This has to remain consistent throughout in the numbering within chapter, and between chapter and chapter. Sub-headings follow relative 'ranking'.

Example:

Capital letters are to be matched by capitals for headings of the same rank, italic by italic.

Similarly, the numbering of headings are to follow such orders like:

I, II,...; A, B ...; (a), (b) ...; (i), (ii) ...; etc.

Different chapters will follow same sequence and style. Specially in books or journals, this has to be under special attention as the various chapters or articles may be by different Authors.

Modern style is to follow numbers, for chapters, sections, or sub-sections, depending on the ranking.

Example:

1.; 1.1; 1.1.1   20., 20.1, 20.1.1

Indentation is also practiced for distinguishing between sections, sub-sections, etc.

1.3.3 Time, Day, Month

1. Abbreviations are used for time of day in text as well as in tables and footnotes. Lowercase is used, no capital letters. Names of days of the week and months begin with capital letter.

8 a.m.	Saturday	Boishakh	February
2-30 p.m.	Wednesday	Muharram	December

2. Months of the year and days of the week are to be spelled out in the text. When used with the date, and only if necessary, months can be abbreviated thus (except for May, June, or July which should be in full)):

    Jan   Feb   Mar   Apr   Aug   Sept   Oct   Nov   Dec

    Sat   Sun   Mon   Tues   Wed   Thurs   Fri

[With the increasing use of computer compose, application of dots and periods after abbreviation have decreased, as in the above examples: Jan Feb Sat Mon, instead of often previously used Jan. Feb. Sat. Wed.]

1.3.4 Use of Dates

1. The common alphanumeric method remains acceptable for calendar dates.

    Example:

    February 21, 2015 or 21 February 2015
    (in place of February 21st, 2015 or February twenty-first, 2015)

Cardinal or ordinal forms are used when the day and month (and no year) only are given.

Example:

July 6   July 6th   the 6th of July   the sixth of July

Time phrases and words are avoided by omission.

Examples:

last year, recently, now, presently, next year are omitted.
Alternatively, actual dates and time are mentioned.
Use of to be published, accepted for publication, awaiting publication, or in press is avoided.

Mention of Dates: Different forms are in practice. The common and simple ones (Oxford style) are thus:

Example:

26 March 1971, without using commas in or after dates.

Months and some abbreviations: Names of months of the year are used in the text in full. In footnotes and similar matters, names of some months are abbreviated, while at least two (March and May) are usually written in full and 'Sept' is used in four letters, instead of normal three.

Examples:

Jan., Feb., Apr., Jun, Jul, Aug., Sept., Oct., Nov., and Dec.

Use of A.D., B.C.

A.D. (anno Domini) follows the year, while B.C. precedes the year.

The University of Dhaka was established in 1921 A.D. That geological era began B.C. 3050.

1.4 PUNCTUATION

1. The period; full stop
2. The comma
3. The semicolon
4. The colon
5. Parentheses
6. Brackets
7. Dashes
8. The hyphen

[For guidelines to other punctuation marks, standard dictionaries and grammar books may be consulted. Only the most commonly used marks are discussed].

1. Period; full stop

1.1 The period is placed within quotation marks.

Example:

> The professor said, "The examination will not take place until the Eid-ul-Fitr holidays are over."

1.2 A period is used after numerals or letters enumerating items in a vertical list.

A period is not used after items in a vertical list unless the items are complete sentences.

Example:

books
houses

Collect all these papers from the seminar:

a) proceedings
b) notes
c) announcements

1.3 A period is used in reference to figure and table numbers.

Example:

See Figure 3.9
See Table 2.5

1.4 The period is placed inside when parentheses or brackets enclose an independent sentence.

Example:

They continued the discussion. "We heard it today."

1.5 The period is placed outside the parentheses when the enclosed matter is part of another sentence.

Example:

The professor already delivered the lecture (the one about bacteria).

1.6 Abbreviations generally take periods. This is however avoided in usages by many institutions, specially in computer applications.

Example:

Dr., Mr., Mrs., St.

1.7 A period is used after a person's initials.

Example:

M. A. Chowdhury
S. K. Sinha
W.B.Yeats

1.8 Acronyms generally do not take periods.

UN, UNESCO, MA, PhD, SAARC, BUET, BAU, BOU, NSU, E-WU, BRACU, AIUB, SEU

[Examples of common Abbreviations and Acronyms are provided elsewhere in this Manual]

1.9 No periods are used for symbols in chemical and physical terms.

Example:

aluminium	Al
zinc	Zn
hydrochloric acid	Hcl

1.10 A period is used inside an end quotation mark.

Example:

The Nobel Laureate reminds: "Peace is to be searched within a group of people first."

2. Comma

A few of the many rules applicable to the use of commas are illustrated here. For the details, one may refer to any standard grammar book.

2.1 For the sake of clarity, commas are used. As they interrupt the flow of a sentence, one has to be careful in using or omitting commas.

2.2 When an element presents incidental or supplementary information which does not affect the essential meaning, it should be set off by a comma or commas.

2.3 Comma is used before 'and' and 'or' in enumerations of three or more items:

Example:

> Large, medium, or small size clothes are available now.
> A Workshop-cum-Seminar was organized by PPD, T&R, and I&PR of Jahangir Nagar University.
> An introductory phrase or clause, specially if it is a long one, is often followed by a comma.
> A small percentage of the total number of publications belongs, as is normal, to academic and research publishing.

2.4 Expressions like namely, that is and for example are usually followed by a comma. They may be preceded by a comma (or a dash or a semicolon or a period).

2.5 The abbreviations i.e. and e.g. should be preceded by a comma (or a dash or an opening parenthesis) but are not followed by a comma.

2.6 A comma is used after words introducing short direct quotations, declarations and direct questions.

Example:

> The Vice Chancellor was heard saying, "Our students are among the very best in the country."

2.7 A comma is used between a surname and a given name or initials if the surname is written first.

Example:

> Khan, Fazle Hassan
> Khan, F.H.

2.8 Commas are used around titles and degrees within the body of a sentence:

Example:

Onimesh Chatterjee, MBBS, FRCS, has been a successful surgeon in our city.

2.9 A comma is used to separate the day of the week from the date and the place from the date.

Example:

Sunday, April 20
London, December 24

2.10 Commas are used to separate all elements in a series or in a list of items.

Example:

Almost all expected participants attended the Meeting, including Rahman, Lewis, Chowdhury, Mahather, and Jayasinghe.

The Publisher's list comprised fiction, non-fiction, children books, religious books, reference books, etc.

3. Semicolon

3.1 When there is a direct relationship between two sentences, they are separated by a semicolon and not by a period. Semicolon is used to separate but not conclude. It is a weak period.

3.2 Semicolon is used if a sharper break is needed and if the break cannot be achieved with a comma.

Example:

He has completed his assignment; he hopes to submit it before the next class.

3.3 Semicolon is replaced by a comma to separate an independent clause from a dependent one.

Example:

He absented himself from the Meeting, which he wished to avoid.

4. Colon

4.1 A colon is used to indicate a formal statement or a speech in dialogue.

Example:

In conclusion, he stated: All of you should come prepared for the lecture ...

4.2 A colon is used to introduce a list or a series.

Example:

The Publishing, Printing and Distribution Division includes these functions: Desktop publishing covering computer compose and typesetting, and layout and design; warehousing (stores); and managing printing by outside presses.

Special courses are offered here every year on: (i) Editing, (ii) Production, (iii) Marketing, etc.

4.3 Colon is used to introduce a list, statement, quotation, or summary.

Example:

The student was asked to submit the following documents: a draft research report, a list of books consulted, names of institutions surveyed, and a list of persons interviewed.

4.4 Colon is used to introduce a clause relating to the preceding clause.

Example:

His party colleagues did not vote for him in the last minute: It was unexpected of them.

4.5 Colon is used to indicate typographic distinctions. For example, colon is used between the volume number and page number in a bibliographic reference.

Example:

Journal of Scholarly Publishing, 32 (2000): 24 – 32.

5. Parentheses

5.1 Parentheses is used to set off explanatory information that does not have a close relationship to the rest of the sentence.

Example:

Most formatting (except for italics, tabs, indents, and superscripts) will be stripped out prior to copyediting.

5.2 Parentheses is used to enclose letters and numerals indicating divisions that run into the text. Only long or complex divisions are numbered.

Example:

> He presented in the seminar a paper that included topics like (1) the art of editing, (2) the process of layout and design, (3) ......

6. Brackets

6.1 Brackets are used to enclose editorial comments, corrections, or explanations.

Example:

> When all faculty members of the University [Bangladesh Open University] attended the Convocation ...

6.2 Brackets are used to enclose the phrases *To be continued* and *Continued from*

Example:

> [Continued from page 25]   [To be continued ...]

7. Dashes

7.1 *Em dash:*

7.1.1   An em dash or a pair of em dashes are used to indicate a sudden break in thought that causes an abrupt change in sentence structure.

7.1.2   Of several kinds of dashes, em dash (or the "long dash") is the most commonly used; when dash is referred in general, it is the em dash.

7.1.3   Often em dash is considered a substitute for the colon, semi-colon or comma although it indicates a more abrupt or emphatic break in the sentence.

Example:

... because we are careless of – or have not undertaken the appropriate research into – the major objectives that one should require of any publishing proposition, they are rarely achieved.

A number of students – boys, girls, young and old – had the same feeling about the postponement of the examination.

7.2 *En dash:*

7.2.1   An en dash is used to indicate continuing dates and times.

Example:

1377 – 1427
8 – 11 a.m.

7.2.2   An en dash is used to indicate a concluding date in the future.
It is half the length of an em dash but longer than a hyphen.

Example:

Albert Einstein (1879-1955)
Kazi Nazrul Islam (1899-1976)

8. Hyphenation

8.1 In modern usage, the trend is to spell compounds as solid words as soon as they have become permanent compounds, and otherwise to spell them as open compounds. The new practice is to avoid use of hyphens.

Example:

day nursery   course book   health food

8.2 Hyphen is used to avoid doubling a vowel or tripling a consonant. Exceptions are there.

Example:

co-ordination   anti-inflammatory   world-wide

8.3 Hyphen is not used when a compound has been accepted as a permanent and solid word.

Example:

payroll   workshop   policymaker   nationwide   breakthrough

8.4 Numerical and some scientific expressions: A hyphen is used with the symbols for chemical elements used in combination with figures.

8.5 Hyphen is not used with superior figures or when the element name is spelled out.

Example:

U-235
uranium 235

U^{23}
^{235}U
H-bomb
U-boat

8.6 A hyphen is used with the adjectives elect or designate as the last element of title.

Example:

chairman-elect
director-designate

8.7 *Prefixes and suffixes:*

8.7.1   A hyphen is used when a prefix appears with a capitalized word or when the term like appears with a proper name.

Example:

Pro-liberation
businessman-like
non-partisan

8.7.2   A hyphen is used to separate a prefix from the root word if the non-hyphenated word would have a different meaning.

Example:

co-op   coop
re-collect   recollect

8.7.3   A hyphen is used to join duplicated prefixes

Example:

> re-reissue
> sub-subheading

8.7.4   Hyphen is used when word fractions are used as adjectives and not used when fractions are nouns.

Example:

> The Party won the Election by a two-thirds majority.
> One third of the electorate cast their votes.

1.5   ITALICIZATION
[In general, common usages are not covered here]

1.5.1   Italicization of scientific terms, foreign words and phrases

1.5.2   Some scientific names and words are italicized.

Example:

> in vivo   in vitro   post mortem

1.5.3   Common scholarly foreign words, Latin words and abbreviations are not italicized.

Example:

> a priori   merci
> i.e.   e.g.   ibid.

1.5.4   Biological and medical terms

The genus and species names are italicized. After using the full name once, the genus name is abbreviated and that also is used in italic.

Example:

Commiphora quadricincta   C. quadricincta
Picea sitchensis
Trichinella spiralis

1.5.5   Other common italicization

a) Titles of books and journals, when they are referred to, or quoted anywhere, are italicized.

Example:

The Chicago Manual of Style
Technology and Scholarly Communication

Journal of Asiatic Society
Journal of Indian Chemical Society

b) In the first use of key terms, which are emphasized for reader's attention, words are italicized. Roman type is used for the subsequent use of the same word.

Example:

The scientist advised on how Newton's Law is to be explained to the students in a simple way.

Both the Biologist and the Environmentalist discussed grave consequences of dumping the lake with debris from the local area.

1.5.6   Italics may not be used for a whole sentence or a paragraph.

1.5.7   When foreign words and phrases sound unfamiliar to readers, italics are used.

Example:

raison d'etat
vis-à-vis
laissez-faire

1.6   PLURALS
[In general, common usages are not covered here]

1.6.1   The plural on the noun in a compound is formed when it is hyphenated with an adverb or a preposition.

Example:

runners-up
hangers-on

1.6.2   The plural is formed on the last word of a compound in which there is no noun.

Example:

put-ons
stand-ins

1.6.3   In abbreviations, the following rules are in practice:

a)   To form the plural, an s is to be added.

Example:

BMWs   777s   MAs   NCOs

b) In case of numerical names ending in a single letter, an apostrophe is used for plurals.

Example:

777A's   777 – 100's

c) An apostrophe is used to make letters and numbers plural.
Example:

> M's and N's are to be avoided in the write-up.
> Bills of 500's become rare during certain days of the month.

1.6.4   If two different plurals are available for the same word, any one may be used, maintaining consistency throughout.

Example:

appendix   formula   index   medium
memorandum   symposium

1.6.5   Examples of Plural forms of some nouns

alumnus	alumni
analysis	analyses
appendix	appendixes or appendices
crisis	crises
criterion	criteria
formula	formulae or formulas

index	indexes (of a book) or indices (in mathematics)
matrix	matrices
medium	mediums or media
memorandum	memorandums or memoranda
millennium	millennia or millenniums
nucleus	nuclei
phenomenon	phenomena
symposium	symposiums or symposia

1.6.6   Plurals of abbreviations for some words like line, note, and page take double letters.

Example:

l., ll   n., nn   p., pp.

As an exception, the plural abbreviation for the word manuscript, s is added as a capital.

Example:

MSS

1.6.7   In the plural form, s is not taken in the abbreviated units of measurement, metric or imperial.

Example:

20 kg   50 lb   10 gm

1.7 INDEFINITE ARTICLES
[Exceptions and uncommon usages are not covered here]

1.7.1 Indefinite article *a* is used before consonant sounds.

Example:

> a Jahangirnagar University graduate
> a science student
> a tourist place

1.7.2 Indefinite article *an* is used before vowel sounds; an is also used before consonants if the first letter takes the help of a vowel for being pronounced or is not pronounced.

Example:

> an umbrella
> an eight-year old child
>
> an M.A.
> an x-ray
>
> an honest person
> an honorary degree

1.8 PLACEMENT AND NUMBERING IN ILLUSTRATIONS AND CAPTIONS

1.8.1 An illustration is placed as close as possible to the first text reference to it. No illustration is inserted before it is referred in the text. Sometimes for ease and cost control, illustrations are placed at the end of the Article or Chapter or in separate page(s). This, however, should be avoided in scientific and academic publications.

1.8.2   When there are more illustrations than one, they are numbered and referred by numbers within the text.

1.8.3   It is preferable to use Arabic numerals, rather than alphabets, numbering them separately even when illustrations are printed side by side and are to be compared.

Example:

Figures 5 and 6, instead of 5a and 5b.

1.9   PHYSICAL QUANTITIES

1.9.1   Numbers under 10 are spelled out; for numbers exceeding 10, numerals are used.
Zero is always spelled out.

Example:

The University of Dhaka is a public institution with about 1,800 faculty members.

In winter, some places in the north of Bangladesh experience zero degree temperature which rises to above 40 degree in the summer.

1.9.2   To express area, distance, length, volume, and other physical measurements in most scientific or technical writing, figures (rather than words) are used.

Example:

12-volt battery
2 cubic ft
3 ems
4 inches

1.9.3   Numbers above four digits are written by using a small space, rather than a comma.

Example:

10 000 (in place of 10,000).

1.9.4   In decimal points, small space is inserted to the right of the decimal point after every three digits when it exceeds four digits.

Example:

29.536 21   32.324 205

1.10   DECIMALS AND PERCENTAGES

1.10.1 Figures are used for decimals and percentages.

1.10.2 For non-scientific text, the word percent or the words per cent are used. For scientific or statistical text, the symbol % is used.

Example:

More than 75 per cent of the articles in the science journals of the universities in Bangladesh are in English, while about 85 per cent of those in the arts journals are in Bengali.

In Minjur sandstone, monocrystalline quartz forms 87% to 99% in all samples, averaging 98%.

1.10.3   A zero is used before the decimal point. Zeros are omitted after decimal point unless necessary to indicate exact measurement.

Example:

0.682
2.5 (instead of 2.50)

1.10.4   Exception is in the use of GPA where two decimal places are required.

Example:

3.00 GPA (instead of 3.0 GPA)

1.11   MISCELLANEOUS

1.11.1   Use of computer and IT words

The following usages related to the computer applications are in practice, concerning capitalization.

Use of capital letters

Example:

the Internet (but internet), (the) Net
CD-ROM
World Wide Web or www or (the) Web
Web site or Web pages
iMac
iPod
iPad
PageMaker

QuarkXPress
Adobe Illustrator
Amazon.com

Avoiding use of capital letters

Example:

e-mail
online
bandwidth
domain

1.11.2 Use of some common Abbreviations

Example:

Av. or Ave. St. Bldg. Pkway. Rd. Sq. N. S. E. W but NW
SW NE SE

bk. = book (pl = bks.)
ed. (eds)   editor (editors)
n.d.   no date
p. (pp.)   page (pages)
rev.   revised
trans.   translator(s)

ch or chap = chapter (pl = chaps.)
col. = column (pl = cols.)
ed. = edition or edited by or editor (pl = eds.)
fig. = figure (pl = figs.)
no. or No. = number (pl = nos. or Nos.)
p. = page (pl = pp)
par. = paragraph
vol. = volume (pl = vols.)
b. = born

d. = died
dept. = department (pl = depts.)
div. = division (pl = divs.)

cc = cubic centimeter
kg = kilogram
m = meter
min = minute
mL = mililiter
h = hour
L = liter

1.11.3 Examples of some common scholarly words in Latin with their English meanings:

cf = confer, compare
e.g. = exempli gratia, for example
et al. = et alii, and others
etc. = et cetera, and others
ibid. = ibidem, in the same place
i.e. = id est, that is
etc. = and so forth
q.v. = quod vide, which see (normally for use with cross-references)
viz. = videlicet, namely

Chapter 2

GUIDELINES ON CITATIONS AND REFERENCING

2.1 Need for citations and referencing

2.1.1 Citations and references are most often essential parts of any academic, scientific or research publication. Confusions and inconsistencies in the use of citations are common with most Authors of research or academic papers. Some special attention to this area is required of such Authors, before submission or publication of their Articles or Papers.

2.1.2 It is natural that Researchers and Authors would make use of many citations and references in their written materials. In the same way, it is obligatory on their part that whenever they use information from other sources, they would make an acknowledgement to those. In addition to Authors' own obligation, also to avoid plagiarism, this will help the readers or users locate the sources easily, in case they require those for further research or writing.

2.1.3 Briefly, a citation makes the readers aware of the source of information the Author would like to quote or provide. The Author cites or refers exactly to the source in the correct and updated way.

2.1.4   Have a good understanding of the kind of source; this will help them decide and find out for themselves further information. Normally, all such references used in the citations are listed at the end of the Article or Chapter.

2.1.5   Among the common forms of documentation (systems of citation and referencing), which may vary a little depending on academic fields, the following Guides are considered standard and useful:

The Chicago Manual of Style
Oxford Style Manual
Harvard Style Guide
MLA (Modern Language Association) Style, used in English or Humanities
CBE (Council of Biology Editors) Style, used in the Life Sciences
CSE (Council of Science Editors) Style
ACS (American Chemical Society) Style
APA (American Psychological Association) Style

2.1.6   Locating appropriate sources: If no satisfactory guidance is readily available, from mentors or supervisors or sources at hand, the researcher may consult one from any recent copy of a standard journal in the library or online. The citations and references used in such a journal may be considered sample or model, provided the publication is a well recognized and reputed one.

2.2 Some basic systems of citations and referencing

2.2.1   The name-and-year system / Harvard Style
2.2.2   The alphabet-number system
2.2.3   The citation-order system

2.2.1 The name-and-year system / Harvard Style

This system has been considered an important and popular standard in citations and referencing.

Citations: In this system, the names of the Authors and the date of publication are cited in the source of information.

Examples:

Ahmed and Hoque (2014) discuss in details about the plants and natural habitats in the area ....

Royal Bengal tigers are at the point of extinction in the Sunderbans, if one recollects their number only three decades ago (Khan, Farah, and Hussain, 2012).

References: The sources are listed at the end of the Article in alphabetical order according to the last name of the first Author, as in the following book and Article. [Dots or periods after initials of Author's name are avoided in today's computer usage].

Examples:

In case of book

Author and date of publication [Title of the book ....], in italic. [City / Place of publication] .... [Name of the Publisher.................]

Ahmed and Hoque (2014). Herbal Plants in the Sunderbans. Dhaka. New Model Publishing House,

In case of Article

Author's last name (and date of publication). "Title of the Article", in roman and not in italic; Title of the Journal, in italic and not in roman .... (volume, and issue, if available, ad page numbers are mentioned).

Khan, MH, Farah, MA, and Hussain, A (2012).

2.2.2   The alphabet-number system

Citations: The source of information is indicated in the Article by giving a number in parentheses; this number will correspond to the one given in the source and will be listed in the alphabetical order in the "References."

Examples:

Regier argues that since parallel publishing in print and online costs more, library budgets will either have to pay more to sustain dual-format journals, choose between them, or cut other purchases (4).

Quandt and Ekman feel that productivity increases [as an effect of IT in universities] are clearly a sine qua non for improvement in the economic situation of universities and libraries, but labor productivity increases are not enough ... (6).

References: The above citations of sources are listed in alphabetical order of Authors and are numbered accordingly, as in the following book:

6. Quandt, RE, and Ekman, R. "Introduction: Electronic Publishing, Digital Libraries, and the Scholarly Environment". In: Technology and Scholarly Communication, Richard Ekman and

Richard E. Quandt, Eds. (Berkeley: University of California Press, 1999).

4. Regier, WG. "Electronic Publishing is Cheaper". In: Technology and Scholarly Communication, Richard Ekman and Richard E. Quandt, Eds. (Berkeley: University of California Press, 1999).

[Note: Other styles are also in practice in the use of similar citations and references]

2.2.3   The citation-order system

Citations: This is normally used in engineering documentation. Here a number is given in brackets that corresponds to the number of the source listed in the order in which they appear in the Article; the source is listed first as [1], second as [2], etc.

Examples:

Bailey and Pick describe that all electrical circuits are ...... and most of those depend on the quality of service rendered by the transmission company [1].

Khan and Chowdhury claim that most universities combine the Departments of Electrical and Electronics as one Department, often adding Applied Physics in the same Department [2].

References: The sources are listed in the order in which they are cited in the Article, as in the following book and Article.

Example:

[1] Bailey, R and Pick, M. "Electrical Circuits: Their Proper Management", Journal of Engineering. Vol. 12, Issue No. 3. pp 36 – 45, 1989.

[2] Khan, AS and Chowdhury, MH. Electrical Circuits and Distribution. Karachi: Taj Publishing House, 2009. 160 p.

NOTE: In science and engineering publications, the last two systems of documentation above are popular: The alphabet-number system, and the citation-order system.

Chapter 3

SOME GENERAL INFORMATION FOR AUTHORS / EDITORS

Some of the following have been discussed in other Sections in this Manual in a slightly different listing; a few are repeated here. It is expected that once the Authors know the various areas of attention, they would be more alert in planning and creating the research, writing the Article or Paper and then finally in producing the Article requiring minimum revision by self and maximum chances of acceptance by the Peer Reviewers.

Separate queries and criteria are applied for marketing and pricing policies and their impact on readership and revenue, if the publication is by a commercial publisher. In today's shrinking academic publishing industry, corporate publishers should also attempt at recovering the costs, if not for profit, making every worthy publication self-supporting. The income earned thus could be diverted to further scholarly publications, making it easier for the usually tight budget of most such publishers.

3.1 Points considered while peer reviewing books for publication

3.1.1   Does the manuscript make a significant contribution to its field?

3.1.2   How important is the subject?

3.1.3   Is the scholarship sound and up to date?

3.1.4   Is the author conversant with the literature of the subject?

3.1.5   Is the organization of the work sound?

3.1.6   Is the style readable? Is the language acceptable, after minor editing?

3.1.7   Would the work benefit by being shortened?

3.1.8   Does it have inaccuracies or omissions?

3.1.9   Does it duplicate or substantially recapitulate other works?

3.1.10   What are the competing books in the field?

3.1.11   To what audience is the manuscript directed?

3.1.12   Do you recommend publication? With or without revisions?

3.2 Ten points to remember by the Editor

1. Read the manuscript more than once. The last time, concentrate on detail.
2. Check the facts. They should be accurate.
3. Enforce the rules. They are the basis of clear communication.
4. Impose consistency. It helps communication.
5. Be thorough.
6. Be neat.
7. Control your pencil. Remember the manuscript is the author's.
8. Check your editing. It may need editing itself.
9. If you aren't sure of anything, look it up. Build the dictionary habit.
10. Don't assume words and numbers are correct just because someone wrote them down.

[*Acknowledgement for Section 3.2:* Ian Montagnes]

3.3 Special features for attention by Authors of Conference Papers

While writing a Paper for Conference, the following features are recommended for noting in particular:

3.3.1 There is enough significance in oral presentation of an academic or research work. This may include both positive outcomes and negative aspects.

3.3.2 While selecting an appropriate Conference, the Researcher may examine these:

a) Announcement on the Call for Papers (do the date, place, topics suit the Participant)?

b) Are the expenses affordable or are there any subsidy or support from anywhere (organizers, other sponsors, or employers)?

c) How wide are the possibilities of useful Networking in the Conference?

d) What chances are there for Publication of the Paper in the Proceedings or elsewhere?

3.3.3 Once the above queries are addressed in favor of the Participant, he or she may proceed with the preparation of writing the Paper thus:

a) Writing and Submitting the Title and the Abstract, and sometimes the Keywords.

b) Writing the Paper, following (a) the Length, (b) Structure, (c) Syntax (words should be simple and audible, sentences should be as simple and as less complex as possible and not long).

3.3.4   3.3.4 Other General Preparation beyond Writing will include:

(a) Time; (b) The Message; (c) Slides and other display materials, if any; (d) Preparedness to handle Questions from the audience.

3.3.5   3.3.5 The Paper in general may follow most practices applicable to a Journal Article. References may be very brief, but a short list may be added for Further Reading.

3.4 Special features for attention by Authors of Journal Articles

3.4.1   A clear conception is required of what the following parts are and how they are prepared in sequence. Some of these are a bit tricky and some may appear overlapping one with the other. With new Authors, most confusion arises from understanding of the difference and similarity of Abstract versus Summary, Conclusion versus Recommendations, Introduction versus Problems and Objectives, etc. One may consult for specific details on these, any standard work of reference appropriate to the particular discipline or specialty. Here only outlines and sequence are provided.

3.4.2   Parts of a Journal Article / Research Paper:

Title
Author name and affiliation
Abstract
Keywords
Introduction
• Issue / Background
• Problems

- Objectives
  - Broad
  - Specific
- Hypotheses
- Rationale
- Scope and Limitations

Literature Review

Methodology: Materials and Methods
Data Collection* (specially in Social Sciences, Business Studies, etc.)

- Primary
- Secondary
- *Sample Size / Sample Frame
- *Questionnaire Development
- Pre-testing

Results or Findings (focusing specific objectives) and Discussion or Analysis
Summary / Conclusion / Recommendations
Acknowledgement
References

[*Acknowledgement* for this Section, 3.4.2: Dr Paul Frazer, Postgraduate and International Student Center, UK]

3.5 Preparing a book: Sequence of items for publication of a book

3.5.1   It should be noted that all of the following are not used in every publication. Some publications may contain all or most.

3.5.2   For the preliminary pages, numbering is preferred in lowercase Roman numerals to distinguish from the main text.

I)   Front matter / Preliminaries (Prelims)

Title page
Copyright notice
    (also containing publisher's address, printer's name and city of printing, notice of authority's approval for publication, etc.)
Dedication (or epigraph), if any
Table of contents
List of illustrations (figures, graphs, photographs, maps)
Captions for illustrative materials
List of Tables
Foreword
Preface
Acknowledgements (if not part of Preface)
Introduction (if not part of text)

II)   Main body of the text (and also preferably of the Chapter or Article)
(must begin on a right-hand or even page)

III) Back matter

Appendix (es) and / or glossary (if any)

Notes (if they form a separate section)
Bibliography (or reference list, in addition to citations, if any, in the specific chapters)
Index (es)

Author information (not an essential part).

3.6 Typical Time Schedule for publication of a book

3.6.1   As an indication to authors, the following may be considered an average standard with a Bangladesh university, taking into consideration most local context. However, depending on the volume of work at the printshop at the time, long summer vacations for authors and editors, time taken for feedback / revision or approval by authors, size and complexity of the book, etc., a medium size, less complicated book should actually be published in 10 to 12 months after the approved manuscript or original is received by the publishing division of a university.

[Comments: In present Bangladesh, most quality printers, copy editors and proofreaders remain extremely busy during November – January for annual Ekushey Boi Mela publications, and during July – October for annual textbook publications. Academic and research publishers should eye for good printers, computer composers and designers during the remaining periods of the year if they wish to proceed properly, even if slow, with desired care. Their production schedule should make provision for such related issues].

3.6.2 **Tentative schedule** (depending on other allied factors, as mentioned above), **in traditional university press or academic publishing**

a) From Author's final manuscript or from Authority's approved typescript to completed copyediting ---- 4 to 6 weeks
b) Author's revisions or feedback ---- 2 to 3 weeks
c) Formatting as per the University's style / making 1st proof ---- 3 to 4 weeks
d) Proofreading by sponsoring Schools, Faculties, Departments or publishing division ---- 2 to 3 weeks
e) Pageproofs or final proofs by typesetting section. ---- 1 to 2 weeks
f) Checking / Approval by Author ---- 2 to 3 weeks
g) Layout and design ---- 2 to 3 weeks
h) Final camera-ready copy by processing section / approval by the publishing division (including ISBN. ---- 2 to 3 weeks)
i) Printing / binding / delivery to distribution center ---- 4 to 5 weeks

----

Average minimum total ---- 27 weeks or approximately 7 months (22 to 32 weeks)

3.7 Sample checklist for editorial and production sections of a publishing department

3.7.1 Originals / manuscripts: Original copy of the manuscript (ms), and not in photocopy, plus the CD or pendrive or any digital version should be received by the publishing unit.--- Manuscript (and disk or digital format) to follow the guidelines meant for authors /

typesetters; the softcopy must match the hardcopy in full. These days, submission of any softcopy properly formatted as per publisher's style or specification is considered an acceptable manuscript.

3.7.2   Title page:

- Title of the book / the journal article
- Full name (s) of the author (s)
- Affiliation of author (s), without abbreviation
- Postal or e-mail address of the author / principal author (if more than one)

3.7.3   In journal articles: Are the section headings, subheadings, etc. in their proper order?

3.7.4   References: Are these in proper sequence and order, following house style? Make sure that the sources mentioned in the reference list correspond with those cited in the text, according to the system followed consistently?

3.7.5   Illustrations / Tables / Graphics: Are they properly labeled, with necessary legends, captions, serial numbers, etc. An additional copy (photocopy) of each figure, plate, map is to be provided.

3.7.6   Pagination: Serial numbering of the complete manuscript (before pagination is made automatic), including figures, tables, attachments, etc. is to be written in pencil (or erasable ink) first.

- In the proof, do the pages have proper running heads (for both even and odd pages, with author, title) and serial auto numbering?

Chapter 4

ROLE, ETHICS AND RESPONSIBILITIES OF EDITORS

4.1 The Editor

THE EDITOR is the: *'Policy maker, gate-keeper, arbiter, author, adviser, manager, upholder of editorial freedom'.*

With so many responsibilities, an Editor has to remain alert and careful about the interests of the Author, the Publisher or the management and the reader.

Group A:

1. It is the Editor in particular who tries to establish and maintain policies and standards for academic journals or any other research publication, as in the case of other publications.

2. The Editor is also to draw up special measures for attracting quality manuscripts as well as for finding out deserving Authors, which may include those who otherwise would have been left unconsidered and unintroduced.

3. It is the Editor again who would assure systems for prompt and constructive evaluation. The Editor will see that prompt and

fair decisions are taken and the same are communicated to the Author without delay.

4. The Editor has to be receptive to new ideas, needs and interests of readers.

5. Again it is the Editor who always tries to improve research as well as manuscripts (often promoting and upholding editorial freedom).

6. The Editor will also decide about the extent of editing -- how much editorial work should be necessary for a particular manuscript.

Group B:

It is the Editor who has often to carry out some of **the Reviewer's tasks**, specially when suitable Reviewers are not available on time. A few such requirements for such an Editor include:

Openness to new ideas, when the Editor (also in the role of a Reviewer) is willing to learn at the same time

- Ability and willingness to evaluate objectively the quality and importance of the article, paper or publication
- Skill to assess validity of conclusions
- Readiness to prepare constructive comments to the help of the Author
- Willingness to maintain confidentiality and integrity of Author's submission
- Preparedness to avoid publishing articles or papers by the Editor in his own journal.

For the improvement of the quality of manuscripts, a few recommendations are re-stressed here:

Training in the preparation of academic and scientific manuscript is to be encouraged in research centers or universities.

- Exclusively designed workshops or short courses in manuscript preparation may be organized from time to time even outside the academia.
- Some senior Authors or mentors are to be involved in reviewing early draft of the manuscript.
- Procedures to be followed for manuscript preparation are to be clearly spelt out in Instructions for Authors (a short list, as an example, is appended elsewhere in this Manu*al)*. These will slightly vary from discipline to discipline, from organization to organization or from publisher to publisher.

Examples:

Some common technical considerations like the following are cared for whilepreparing a manuscript by new Authors:

- Double spacing throughout
- Each chapter, section or a component to begin from a new page
- Following the sequence in this order: Title page (including mention of author/s with affiliation), abstract and keywords, text, acknowledgements, references, Tables, legends, etc.
- Each Table is to be in separate page
- Declaration or confirmation of permission to reproduce previously
- published material (the journal may require enclosure of transfer of copyright and other forms).

The Authors as well as the Editors may like to double-check if answers to some of the following are in the affirmative. If not, the Authors may try again to improve their manuscript, specially in the case of journals:

- Is the topic of the paper or manuscript important and suitable for readership
- Is it an original study or is it confirmed that the submission is an important study
- Is it a well-designed, well-conducted or well-analyzed study
- Does it meet high ethical standards
- Are the results clear (positive or negative) and appropriately interpreted
- Are the conclusions straightforward and based on results
- Is the submission well-written and concise and with appropriate tables and figures

4.2 Of Editors and their integrity: Some editorial tasks, freedom and risk

- Often some differences may appear between publishers or owners or top management and the Editors of academic or scientific journals.
- The common objective of both groups remains the same: Timely and quality publication of their journal or work.
- To minimize conflicts of interest or implementation of policies, and also to have a broader perspective from all sides, an Editorial Advisory Board is desirable. This Board will be independent of all stakeholders, and is likely to contribute to resolving issues of conflict whenever these occur, and to establishing and maintaining editorial policy.
- While publishers or owners may like to give more importance to business and management aspects, it is the editorial team which will be expected to have complete

authority for determining the editorial content of the publication.

- Editorial freedom has to be reflected here in a strong manner, if necessary making their position risky. Instances are not rare when Editors were found to have left their job or to have been terminated, when they had to respect their own academic or professional integrity.

4.3 Editor's respect to confidentiality and Author's rights

- In case of peer reviewed journals, where most articles are read by one or more experts, none being part of the editorial team, some reviewing procedures are mentioned to them and sometimes to the Authors too. Scientific and academic journals usually disclose their policies to the Authors publicly as instructions or guidelines. This helps all concerned --- readers, potential authors and new reviewers.

- Editors keep in mind that until publication, and specially while in the hands of peer reviewers, the manuscripts of authors, their status such as receipt, content, opinions of the reviewers, will not be disclosed to anyone other than the Authors themselves and the concerned reviewers.

- All kinds of information including interim review results or opinions are parts of the 'privileged communication' that are authors' private property. Hence Editors and their staff will treat all such stages and communication as authors' rights and the Editors or their staff shall desist from disclosing publicly their decisions in process or their status. They will not discuss or share authors' ideas with anyone else, without the clear permission of the Editor in charge.

- Retention of copies of the rejected articles or manuscripts is also prohibited.

- Even when comments are made with reviewers' signature or identity to the editor, this is not to be disclosed to the Author without the Reviewers' consent.
- It is the Author whose reputation and career may depend on some particular reviews, publication of their work, or their disclosure to anyone other than the Author himself.
- Since the Editor is the executor of all processes in between, assisted by his team, he is fully entrusted by the Author. The Editor is committed to honor the trust of non-disclosure of the results of the authors' academic or scientific or creative work or of any information that might encourage other authors in similar research to proceed and to benefit from unpublished findings or ideas or to misrepresent any part of those in advance. Confidentiality is to be maintained till publication, or even if the manuscript is rejected.

4.4 Ten rules in editing for detail

Various rules are in practice. These differ from Editor to Editor, from Publisher to Publisher, from Author to Author. Starting from specialized terms to unusual spellings, capitalization and hyphenation, some Authors would insist on following their style on these. For all, no single style book can be used. Institutions and universities therefore create and adopt their own which has to be followed whenever differences occur.

One expert (Montagnes,1991) has summarized 10 rules in editing for detail:

1. Read the manuscript more than once. The last time, concentrate on detail.
2. Check the facts. They should be accurate.
3. Enforce the rules. They are the basis of clear communication.

4. Impose consistency. It helps communication.
5. Be thorough.
6. Be neat.
7. Control your pencil. Remember the manuscript is the Author's.
8. Check your editing. It may need editing itself.
9. If you aren't sure of anything, look it up. Build the dictionary habit.
10. Don't assume words and numbers are correct just because someone wrote them down.

4.5 Some Guidelines for Peer Review [Also of use to potential Authors, Editors, and Readers]

1. **On the content and structure of the manuscript**, the following questions are to be checked by a Reviewer (or also by an Editor, if he works partly for the Reviewer in the latter's non-availability in time), among some more:

2. In majority of the standard scientific and academic journals, common procedures for external (non- inhouse) review are more or less the same. Some do not deviate from these but introduce a few more to suit their specific purpose. As an example, some of these are well outlined for adoption by a standard medical journal from a comparatively less advanced country. These may also be followed, and are mostly being followed already, by other developing countries for their respective scientific and academic publications:

2.1. Is the manuscript or Article a new and original contribution
2.2. Is it largely confirmatory
2.3. Are the methods sound and adequately described

2.4. Are the conclusions and interpretations sound and justified by the data

2.5. Is the abstract accurate and informative

2.6. Are the references correctly cited

2.7. Does the title adequately reflect the content?

3. The above are also summed up in a slightly different format, with **Editors and Reviewers** requiring to check:

3.1. How much or what proportions of the manuscript or Article should be **expanded, condensed, combined** or **deleted** altogether.

3.2. Whether all Tables and Figures are clearly labeled and well planned, and if these are too complex or unnecessary.

3.3. Whether the results stated in the text of the Article or manuscript are easily verifiable by examining and cross-verifying with Tables and Figures, among a few other items.

3.4. Whether the methods followed in the Article are appropriate, current, described clearly enough for others to repeat, if necessary.

3.5. Whether the major contents of the Article or Paper reflect consistently and accurately the appropriate use of the title, abstract, key words, introduction and conclusions.

4. **For the Reviewers** as well as for the Editors acting as Reviewers, special attention is needed for the following:

- Identification of important contribution of the Article or Paper
- Major strengths and **weaknesses, specially noting organization and study, cohesiveness** of argument, length relative to the number of new ideas and information, conciseness and style.

Peer Reviewing:

In another way, Editors' evaluation of the merits of a submitted manuscript may include these features – originality, design, results of the study, the composition of the manuscript, and its interest to readers of a particular journal or publication.

Use of References:

Some standard practices of the use of references:

- These are numbered consecutively in the order in which they are first mentioned in the text. References are identified in text, Tables and legends by Arabic numerals in parentheses.
- Use of abstracts as references is avoided. It is always desirable that the references are verified by the Author against the original documents.
- When there are a few Authors, the first three to four Authors are followed by et al.
- When Articles are not in English, standard journals translate the title to English, enclosing the translation in square brackets, and adding an abbreviated language designator.

[Acknowledgement for this Section in general: *9ᵗʰ International Conference of Science Editors, June 8-10,1998.* Sharm-Al-Sheikh, Egypt. *Workshop Papers* and Notes by the present Author who was also a participant in the above Meet].

4.6 Sample checklist for editorial and production sections of a publishing department

4.6.1 Originals / manuscripts: Original copy of the manuscript (ms), and not in photocopy, plus the CD or pendrive or any digital version should be received by the publishing unit.--- Manuscript (and disk or digital format) to follow the guidelines meant for authors / typesetters; the softcopy must match the hardcopy in full. These days, submission of any softcopy properly formatted as per publisher's style or specification is considered an acceptable manuscript.

4.6.2 Title page:

- Title of the book / the journal article
- Full name (s) of the author (s)
- Affiliation of author (s), without abbreviation
- Postal or e-mail address of the author / principal author (if more than one)

4.6.3 In journal articles: Are the section headings, sub-headings, etc. in their proper order?

4.6.4 References: Are these in proper sequence and order, following house style? Make sure that the sources mentioned in the reference list correspond with those cited in the text, according to the system followed consistently?

4.6.5 Illustrations / Tables / Graphics: Are they properly labeled, with necessary legends, captions, serial numbers, etc. An additional copy (photocopy) of each figure, plate, map is to be provided.

4.6.6 Pagination: Serial numbering of the complete manuscript (before pagination is made automatic), including figures, tables, attachments, etc. is to be written in pencil (or erasable ink) first.

- In the proof, do the pages have proper running heads (for both even and odd pages, with author, title) and serial auto numbering?

Chapter 5

PLAGIARISM / COPYRIGHTS / INTELLECTUAL PROPERTY / FAIR USE

Terms like plagiarism / originality / copyrights / permission / intellectual property / fair use relate to authorship and ethics. In the academia or in any research field, ethical standards are to be given due importance. To follow such standards, the following points may be noted.

5.1 Every piece of research or academic work is expected to be original in thought, expression, writing and style. However, it becomes part of presentation and knowledge-sharing to make use of other researches or original works. In such cases, plagiarism is to be avoided by adopting several practices. One such essential practice is due acknowledgement to the earlier work or researcher. This could be for words or ideas or long description.

5.2 In practice, plagiarism means copying another's work or borrowing someone else's original ideas.

Stealing or passing off the ideas or words of another person as one's own without crediting the source and to present the same as new and original. Such copying or borrowing of an existing source without acknowledgement or permission amounts to an act of fraud. It involves both stealing someone else's work and lying about it afterward.

5.3 But can words and ideas really be stolen?

According to U.S. law, the answer is yes. The expression of original ideas is considered intellectual property and is protected by copyright laws, just like original inventions. Almost all forms of expression fall under copyright protection as long as they are recorded in some way (such as a book or a computer file).

5.4 Penalties

For violation of ethical standards in the academia, heavy penalties are in practice, specially in the countries that are members of the UNESCO or signatory to the Copyright Conventions. Such penalties may include: Suspension or termination from service, cancellation of the research work or the research degree, downgrading the rank and status of an academic in his place of work, public defamation through media, rejection of candidature in any academic or research job, shame to and avoidance of the violating academic by the students, colleagues and the community.

5.5 All of the following are considered plagiarism:

- turning in someone else's work as the copyist's own
- copying words or ideas from someone else without giving credit
- failing to put a quotation in quotation marks
- giving incorrect information about the source of a quotation
- changing words but copying the sentence structure of a source without giving credit

- copying so many words or ideas from a source that it makes up the majority of the copyist's work, whether credit is given or not.

Most cases of plagiarism can be avoided, however, by citing sources. Simply acknowledging that certain material has been borrowed and providing the audience with the information necessary to find that source is usually enough to prevent plagiarism. [Refer to the Section on Citation in this book for more information on how to cite sources properly.]

Chapter 6

SHORT DESCRIPTION ON A FEW OTHER PUBLISHING RELATED ISSUES

6.1 E-Publishing and e-Journals: Their Specialty and Challenges

'Journals that are of scholarly or intellectual nature and are accessible via electronic transmission are known as electronic journals or ejournals or e-journals.'

Electronic journals are normally published on the Web. They are a specialized form of electronic document. Their objective is to provide material for academic research and study. For this, formatting of the e-journals is more or less like Articles in traditional printed journals.

A brief discussion follows about the introduction and popularity as well as challenges of electronic journals:

- Electronic journal has become a tool, often as in addition to, and not as a substitute to, printed journals.
- e-journals are expanding popularity as these are speedier and less costly than traditional print journals.
- Impact of e-journals is growing.

Advantages include: Facilities for rapid corrections, correspondence and technical debates; commentary and discussion groups;

provision of linkages to other sites; issues of quality, particularly with updating ease.

- Another great advantage of the e-journals or e-publications is the convenient and fast facility for citation, archiving, and indexing.
- Some editorial challenges however keep on expanding, including: Finding out comparability of texts and illustrations; decisions by Editor or Reviewer or Mentor in addition to or exclusion of text, tables and figures to Articles; responsibilities of Authors and Editors for content; timing of online publication versus print publication; lifespan of electronic publication; even consideration of electronic publication as publication.
- Other limitations include those for Authors and Editors who have to pay proper attention to: Adaption to the new mode of publication, involving additional works for both Author and Editor; necessity for suitable technological support, including expertise, equipment and resources.
- Electronic publishing, the basic requirements of traditional publishing process do not change. The same importance is given to proper editing, attractive and readable formatting, proofreading, indexing, marketing, protection of copyright, collection of usage fees and payment of royalties, etc. In practice, all other fulfillment services are provided for effecting the dissemination of published information between the author and the user.
- The organizational structure of the text follows usual paragraphs, sections, etc. Publication formats take care of clear displays, and not that much 'the geometric look of printed pages'.

[*Acknowledgement* for part of this Section 6.1: Wikipedia]

6.2 Self-publishing

It is the process of publishing almost fully handled by the Author, without involving any third-party publisher. A system has been developed by many agencies to help the self-publisher in following the procedures, step by step. It is less time taking, and is under full control of the self-publisher in writing, editing, production, and distribution.

In recent years, with the advent of online facilities, self-publishing has widened its participation by enthusiastic and fast Authors. The cover design and formatting of the interior, as well as pricing and marketing of the publication are all carried out by the Author or Self-publisher. The Author or Self-publisher can also outsource the publishing activity partly or fully to agencies offering such services at reasonable cost. E-books are mostly self-published. Books are printed or made available in hardcopies or standard books on demand, thus avoiding large print runs, warehousing and distribution.

6.3 Style Guide or Manual of Style

A **style guide** or **manual of style** is a set of standards for the writing and design of documents. These may be for general use or for a specific publication. A style manual or style guide helps the Author and Editor in the **improvement and standardization of communication** and 'ensures **consistency** within a document and across multiple documents and enforces best practice in usage and in language composition'. A style manual also indicates ways for the proper use of 'visual composition, orthography (including spelling, capitalization, hyphenation, and other punctuation), and typography'.

A style guide or manual contributes in **academic, scientific and technical documents,** specially for the enforcement of best practice in ethics like authorship, research ethics, and disclosure as well as in pedagogy like exposition and clarity, and in compliance of technical and regulatory measures.

Publishers' own house rules or style

Standard publishers introduce their own house style which are mandatorily followed by their Authors. Basically they guide on their rules for language use, like those in spelling, italics and punctuation.

It becomes necessary to **revise and update** style guides periodically. Some revise annually (like the *AP Stylebook),* some revise these every 10 or 20 years like the manuals by Chicago, APA, and ASA.

A few **commonly used style manuals** are:

Oxford Style or *New Oxford Style Manual (Reference)* (for general use)
Chicago style or *The Chicago Manual of Style* (since 1906, now in its 16th edition) (for general use)
Harvard Style or *Harvard System of Referencing* (for general use)
APA Style or American Psychological Association Style
ASA Style or American Sociological Association Style
CSE Style or Council of Science Editors Style
ACS Style or American Chemical Society Style
CBE Style or Council of Biology Editors
MLA Style or Modern Language Association Style
AMA Style or American Medical Association Style

Business Style Handbook

Bluebook Style by Georgetown University Law Center (which is now in its 19th edition)

[Brief bibliographic notes on the above manuals are available at the end of this book].

Besides, **Website** style guides are now used; these particularly cover a publication's visual and technical aspects, along with text. Example: *The Columbia Guide to Online Style*

In addition to those mentioned earlier, different style guides and manuals are consulted **internationally or regionally.** Examples are: For the international reference: *ISO 215 Documentation – Presentation of contributions to periodicals and other serials,*

For Europe, Australia and Canada, popular Manuals are:

Europe

Interinstitutional Style Guide—this encompasses 23 languages across the European Union.

Australia

Style Manual: For Authors, Editors and Printers by Snooks & Co.

Canada

The Canadian Style: A Guide to Writing and Editing: by Dundurn Press, Toronto and Oxford

In **Bangladesh or South Asia, or in the Middle East,** either American or British styles and standards are normally followed with some adaptation to suit individual country's specific requirements. New style manuals are now being published for these regions. [Example: the present compilation].

Chapter 7

BIBLIOGRAPHY: SELECTED BOOKS ON STYLE AND REFERENCE

7.1 General Reference
7.2 For specific academic disciplines

7.1 General Reference

- Oxford Advanced Learner's Dictionary of Current English
- Merriam – Webster's Collegiate Dictionary
- The Chicago Manual of Style [16th edition]
- Judith Butcher's Copy-editing: The Cambridge Handbook
- Kate Turabian's A Manual for Writers of Term Papers, Theses, and Dissertations
- The Canadian Style: A Guide to Writing and Editing
- Karen Judd's Copyediting: A Practical Guide
- Oxford Dictionary for Writers and Editors
- Author Handbook: University of Columbia Press
- University of Minnesota: Style Manual
- Ian Montagnes' Editing and Publication: A Training Manual

7.2 For specific academic disciplines

7.2.1 *Humanities, Social Sciences and Sciences in general*

- A Manual for Writers of Research Papers, Theses, and Dissertations, 7th edition: Chicago Style for Students and Researchers, by Kate L. Turabian. (Commonly called "Turabian style".)
- MLA Handbook for Writers of Research Papers by Joseph Gibaldi. (Commonly called "MLA style".)
- Publication Manual of the American Psychological Association by the American Psychological Association. Primarily used in social sciences. (Commonly called "APA style".)
- AMA Manual of Style: A Guide for Authors and Editors by the American Medical Association. Primarily used in medicine. (Commonly called "AMA style".)
- Scientific Style and Format: The CSE Manual for Authors, Editors, and Publishers by the Council of Science Editors. Used widely in the natural sciences, especially the life sciences. (Commonly called "CSE style".)
- ACS Style Guide: Effective Communication of Scientific Information, 3rd ed. (2006), edited by Anne M. Coghill and Lorrin R. Garson, and ACS Style Guide: A Manual for Authors and Editors (1997). Primarily used for the physical sciences, such as physical chemistry, physics, and related disciplines. (Commonly called "ACS style".)
- IEEE Style: Mainly for Engineering Sciences.

7.2.2 *Business*

- The Business Style Handbook, An A-to-Z Guide for Effective Writing on the Job, by Helen Cunningham and Brenda Greene.
- The Gregg Reference Manual, by William A. Sabin.

7.2.3   *Law*

The Bluebook Uniform System for Citation, developed jointly by the faculty at Harvard and Columbia Universities' Schools of Law.

7.2.4   *Journalism*

- The Associated Press Stylebook, by the Associated Press (AP).
- The New York Times Manual of Style and Usage, by The New York Times

More materials in plenty and in detail are available on various websites on writing, editing, publishing, self-publishing, publishing online, specially for those who wish to get away from traditional publishing in print.

Some such reference tools for **online or e-publishing** are:

- Janice Walker and Todd Taylor. The Columbia Guide to Online Style.
- Chris Barr and the Yahoo! Editorial Staff. The Yahoo! Style Guide: The Ultimate Sourcebook for Writing, Editing and Creating Content for the Web.
- Chicago Manual of Style. [16th edition, 2010].

Any other authentic book of reference by any reputed international publisher may also be consulted.

[*Additional sources* consulted by and available with the present Compiler – Author that may be provided on request are:

GENERAL: Worksheets / Notes from Lectures / Courses attended or participated by the present Author / Compiler, specially at Oxford University (UK), Stanford University (USA), Simon Fraser University (Canada), and Open University of UK.

SPECIFIC:

- on Desktop Publishing for Academics, participated at Simon Fraser University, Vancouver, Canada, 1995;
- on Advance Publishing for Professionals, at Stanford University, California, USA, 1983;
- on Production, Design, Marketing and Rights sales / Copyrights, at different seminars and discussion sessions and in international Book Fairs, specially in Karachi (1970), Frankfurt (1973, 1975, 1978), New Delhi (1976, 1979), Kolkata (several times), Belgrade (1978), Bahrain (1983), Cairo (1993), Thessaloniki, Greece (1994), New Zealand (2004), West Indies (2006), Cambridge (2007); London (2008) ; and during different visits / discussions in Tokyo, Singapore, Hong Kong, Kuala Lumpur, Colombo, Kathmandu, Paris, The Hague, Toronto, Vancouver, Washington DC, New York, Boston, and other academic and publishing places;
- on Advance Practices in Publishing Management at Oxford University, UK, 1973.
- Course Plan for a Masters Level program on Academic and Research Writing and Editing prepared by the present Author / Compiler, 1995 and revised in 2005 / 2012].

Chapter 8

GLOSSARY OF A FEW COMMON TERMS USED BY AUTHORS AND PUBLISHERS

ISBN: International Standard Book Number is a numerical commercial book identifier. It helps in identifying the product and assists in the selling of the book.
Usually, ISBN is assigned to each edition and variation.

It comprises 13 digits and has been in use sine 1970.

Example:

ISBN 265-2-15-246322-0

ISSN: International Standard Serials Number is used for identifying periodicals or serials worldwide. Normally it is in printed form, but may also be in other media (including online).

ISSN consists of 8 digits. Serials include: Journals, magazines, newspapers, annuals, proceedings, etc.

Example:

ISSN 1198-9742

ROYALTY: This is a payment made by the Publisher to the Author for ownership of the creation or asset.

Royalty is basically in the form of a percentage of net revenues earned from the use of a publication and is on a fixed price, usually being the published price per unit sold.

GLOSSARY: 'It is an alphabetical list of terms in a particular domain of knowledge with the definitions for those terms.'

Glossary appears at the end of the book.

Glossary covers words that are common, or specialized or newly introduced.

INDEX: It is more or less a detailed alphabetical listing of names, places, and topics along with the numbers of the pages on which they are mentioned or discussed.

Index is placed as a back matter or in pages at the end of the book.

PRELIMS OR PRELIMINARY PAGES or FRONT MATTER:
These are all texts that appear before the main body of the text in a publication, such as: Title of the publication, Author, Publisher, Details about Copyright, Printer with address, Year and Place of publication, Dedication, Foreword or Preface, Introduction, Table of Contents, etc.

These are also termed Front Matter.

END MATTER or BACK MATTER: All that appears after the main text, at the end of the book, like: Glossary, Index, Bibliography, About the Author, etc.

Chapter 9

APPENDIX

9.1 Introduction to a Workshop for University Faculty on Research and Academic Writing for Journals and Conferences

A WORKSHOP FOR UNIVERSITY FACULTY ON RESEARCH AND ACADEMIC WRITING FOR JOURNALS AND CONFERENCES: *An Introductory Lecture*

1. At one point we were asked how and who actually will learn about the 'style' or techniques or standards and practices of writing in the academic or research world. The feeling in general was -- if they know about the research methods and if they can conduct research, they can very well put those or their results in black and white.

   Our answer is: If that is the case, why are there so few publications in the form of single-authored journal articles or peer-reviewed conference papers. In the academic world, publications cannot be without research and research will loose its significance if the work is not published. That is why, a common message for the academics and researchers, specially since the early twentieth century, has been: 'Publish or perish'. First, research has to be carried out following its own methodology. After that, these have to be disseminated or placed before the wide world through writings in journals or presentations face-to-face, now often online too. That is how we share knowledge. And knowledge - dissemination in the institutions of higher education cannot be only through teaching in the classrooms. It is much beyond that, if successful and in-depth spread of knowledge to the young undergraduate or graduate students has to be achieved with some level of originality in ideas and style. It is writing again, preceded of course by research, that will judge the young teachers' performance and achievements which will result in further promotion in his career, recognition in his field, and more confidence – building in fulfilling his routine responsibilities.

2. This is one reason why a research degree becomes essential for university teachers. Such a degree, like PhD, is common for all promotion-seeking (and also knowledge-seeking) Faculty. And which member of the Faculty does not want to attain that? Exceptions are there too, where regular and quality research works have been conducted, numerous quality writings have been published and due recognition has been accorded, without research degrees. We wish to proceed with general practices of researching, writing and publishing.

3. We have seen how shy or unnecessarily incapable a large section of such less experienced but otherwise well qualified teachers feel till writing and submission of an Article to a Journal or a Paper to a Conference. Many a time their contributions are rejected outright (though with polite thanks for the interest shown in the Journal or Conference) or are sent back with reviewers' comments. To address such observations again, the original writer or author often faces frustration and the revision task might become as (or sometimes more) difficult as writing a fresh Article or Paper itself.

4. For us, we are concerned with the young teachers in general, with those who have spent their first three to five years or a few more years in classroom-teaching, without much confidence as they are yet to earn a PhD or similar research degree, or are yet to be known as an Author through some peer-reviewed or standard journals or as a presenter of any paper in some respectable local, regional or international academic Meet. While on the one hand, these serious, career-seeking university teachers try their best to perform well with their students, on the other they wish to be better recognized in their own profession. In both cases, contribution of research and writing or research and publication will continue to have a great impact.

5. To our knowledge, not much has been done, formally or informally, in the field of training or teaching on the methods and standards of writing for academic or research purposes. It is only through individual attempts by supervisors, mentors or seniors that their very few PhD or MPhil or Graduate students per year or per semester are guided in conducting research, followed by writing. What about the rest – the vast multitude of new, budding and non-research-degree holding Lecturers, Assistant Professors or even Associate Professors who must go higher up in the minimum period, before their energy or opportunity is 'exhausted' or before their other commitments in the family or academic or professional world compel diversion.

6. Our perception is: A systematic and scientific approach in training the promising and willing university teachers (where the number is increasing in a rapid way, with the growth of universities in our country, and rightly so) has become necessary in the present competitive world. More and more quality writing by younger scholars will encourage more and more journals and other research works to be published in time before results become outdated.

7. So far, writing in our universities has not been considered with the importance it deserved. Some good journals have seen light of the day, often with irregular frequency though. Some others have been published in a sub-standard quality, sorry to mention. In the latter group, neither norm, style or minimum quality in the written text has been followed, nor has there been respect to standard academic publishing practices. This is all mainly due to ignorance, or absence of skill, or sheer negligence by the would-be author himself or due to non-availability of the time, attention and guidance often voluntarily required of a senior, supervisor or mentor. The last act has to continue in a more regular manner -- though simply impractical or very difficult, with the otherwise valuable time, workload and pressing responsibilities that seniors and qualified ones are entrusted with. In its absence, a systematic, innovative approach is needed.

8. Who will take up the task? Who has the time, energy, willingness to sacrifice for the 'trainees' or 'lifelong learners' through a faster process? This makes it all the more desirable to plan, run and develop such programs as the present Workshop, for larger groups. Imagine the number of annual intake of 'Teachers' in 100 or more universities of the country, think of those Teachers who have entered their noble and respectable profession some 3 to 5 years ago, but who could not manage time and skill to research or writing practices, beyond their classroom teaching, examination conducting, strict reporting and some 'non-academic' works. In the private universities, young Teachers are often overloaded to 'justify' their comparatively 'attractive' emoluments or packages. In public universities, quality or lifelong learning while teaching is often interrupted by 'other important and mundane works' (discussion of which is out of scope here).

9. How do we resolve then?

   Our small organization, Center for Development through Open Learning, Publishing and Communication (CEDOLPC) is a new (only less than 10 -year old), research, training and development center focusing also on academic writing and publications. So far we have remained involved in ICT-enabled education, open learning and development works, occasionally related to such 'trainings', orientation or introductory workshops including those at universities. Now some of our well qualified associates (both very senior and junior alike) -- academics, researchers and professionals have some more time to spare during our second and current five years (2011 – 2015). They can now concentrate on similar projects as the present one, concerning service to higher education through Faculty Development, among a few other programs. This will be specially through Research, Writing and Publication. Still we believe, 'small is beautiful' and our aim would be to make CEDOLPC a center of excellence in course of time; we will proceed slow, but trying to remain steady. We hope to move forward methodically.

10. To brief our promising Participants about the above, we have designed our Workshop in a way so that they may briefly know something of all relevant items in writing and researching, while they would be oriented to some detailed aspects of a few more necessary issues related to writing and research techniques and standards. To achieve this, we intend to cover some of the following, a few in some details, and a few through some practicals or assignments on the spot.

10.1 Writing Techniques / Publication and Presentation Procedures will include:

- Basics of Academic and Research Writing
- Standards and Practices in Journals and Conferences
- Parts of a Journal Article: Title / Authorship and Affiliation / Abstract / Keywords / Introduction / Literature Review / Main Discussion / Results / Conclusion / Referencing and Citations
- Essentials of Conference Papers
- Acknowledgement
- Referencing system

10.2 Research Methodology will include:

- Basics of Research
- Qualitative Research and Its Application (and short briefing on Quantitative Research)
- Research Design / Method
- Tools and Approaches
- Laboratory experiments / Surveys / Data collection
- Findings or Results and their Discussion / Analysis.
- Conclusion / Recommendations

11. An exclusive, more detailed two-week Workshop may be in the evenings only has been suggested by some previous participants. We are exploring that too.

12. Our efforts could be doubled or multiplied if universities and other interested institutions come forward in a collaborative spirit, if such basic now and advanced or more detailed trainings later are considered essential and until full-fledged training centers of the kind are in place. It is with this hope that we have tried to initiate the current 2-Day Workshop with

active cooperation of eight public and private universities. In our five or more Sessions we will have support from at least five senior academics of reputed public universities of Dhaka and Sylhet, and my humble self, to assist you in knowing about the techniques, standards and practices of Writing and partly researching so that you could continue to learn more and then practise.

13. You may be aware, some three or four universities in Dhaka have already undertaken in-house teaching learning or professional development centers or institutes that mainly deal with orientation of very new teachers specially in the teaching methods and student matters for their own institutions. That is fine. But what about those who already spent some years of their creative, inspiring and formative years, in some cases five to seven years, and have not been in a position to publish any journal article or take part in any research work. Result, they could not be promoted on merit to Assistant or Associate level even after the expected period of sincere service. Programs such as the current one to capacity building for teachers are required more and more and for longer duration. Such programs will enable them to really learn what will allow them to effective practice in research and writing --- the strong ladder to rise up in the academic arena.

14. In a study by some senior academics, it was revealed that 40 % of the faculty members had zero publications in national journals. To speak of international journals, as high as 50% of the faculty had no publication at all while 22% had only one publication.

15. Incentives for the faculty in the universities should not be on the number of courses one may teach (sometimes it is four or more per semester). These incentives should include what and

how many research works or knowledge creation works and their dissemination through publications have been carried out by that faculty member.

[Acknowledgement: Introductory Lecture by the present Author on the Why and How of a Workshop for University Teachers on Academic and Research Writing for Journals and Conferences, held at Shahjalal University of Science & Technology, Sylhet, Bangladesh in August 2014].

9.2 Example of part coverage of related sub-topics on academic and scientific writing

[Examples of topics and issues covered in some of the Workshops on Academic and Research Writing, particularly for Journals and Conferences, and directed by the present Author (organized by his Center for Development through Open Learning, Publishing and Communication, CEDOLPC, Dhaka) and presented in slides in various Workshops by different Resource Persons at various universities in Bangladesh are reproduced here].

Appendix

Example:1

22 August 2014: Day 1 // University Teachers' Workshop (22-23 Aug'14) at SUST, Sylhet

INTRODUCTION TO
ACADEMIC AND RESEARCH WRITING
FOR JOURNALS / CONFERENCES

by Manzurul Islam
Chairman / Chief Consultant, CEDOLPC, Dhaka
and
Former Adviser, Bangladesh Open University and
Southeast University, Dhaka

1

1. INTRODUCTION

1.1 BASICS of academic and research writing including their meanings at both conceptual and operational levels (in the context of Bangladesh)

Conceptual level

Operational level

2

Kinds of Writing

1.2 Kinds of Writing

➢ Academic
➢ Research
➢ Scientific
➢ Scholarly / Learned

3

WHY to write

1.3 WHY to write

➢ To publish (or 'perish')
➢ To disseminate
➢ To share knowledge
➢ To qualify for promotion
➢ To be recognized nationally, globally
➢ To remain self-satisfied and self-confident

4

*Redundancies and Repetitions
REDUNDANCIES in any quality academic publication, are to be removed
Examples of few common redundant words and phrases that should be revised: Examples of some common REDUNDANCIES

(absolutely) necessary	(close) proximity	(new) beginning
attach (together)	connect (together)	(now) pending
(actual) facts	collaborate (together)	(new) recruit
ATM (machine)	disappear (from sight)	outside (of)
assemble (together)	each (and every)	(past) experience
autobiography (of his or her own life)	(exact) same	(present) incumbent
(basic) fundamentals	(foreign) imports	(past) history
(brief) summary	(future) plans	present (time)
blend (together)	(former) graduate	PIN (number)
biography (of his--or her--life)	few (in number)	plan (ahead)
(completely) eliminate	(former) veteran	repeat (again)
circle (around)	filled (to capacity)	reason (why)
(completely) filled	(free) gift	(twelve) noon or midnight
circulate (around)	(final) conclusion	(two equal) halves
(careful) scrutiny	(general) public	(ultimate) goal
classify (into groups)	join (together)	undergraduate (student)
cash (money)	(joint) collaboration	warn (in advance)
		whether (or not)

REPETITIONS are to be avoided or in case of emphasis or learner's interest in the academic texts (if these are considered essential), these should be minimized as much as possible.
© Dr. Manzurul Islam, 2014

2. ACADEMIC and RESEARCH WRITING
2.1 Language:

➤ Grammar and Syntax
➤ Spelling
➤ Punctuaton
➤ Capitalizaton
➤ Redundancies and Repetitions

© Dr. Manzurul Islam, 2014 5

2. ACADEMIC and RESEARCH WRITING (continued...)

2.3 Writing for a Journal (= Article)

➤ Abstract
➤ Keywords
➤ Introduction
➤ Materials and Methods
➤ Results and Discussion or Analysis
➤ Conclusion
➤ Acknowledgement
➤ Referencing / Citations

© Dr. Manzurul Islam, 2014 8

2. ACADEMIC and RESEARCH WRITING (continued...)

2.2 Style / Presentation
➤ Simple
➤ Comprehensible
➤ Clear, concise, consistent and complete
➤ information
➤ Meaningful

© Dr. Manzurul Islam, 2014

2. ACADEMIC and RESEARCH WRITING

2.4 Writing for a Conference (= Paper):

- Does it differ from a Journal's
- What kind of introductory para / references to other presentations in the Conference already made or to be made
- Points of emphasis / or issues not covered earlier / or countering some comments or observations in other presentations
- For oral presentation or discussion on salient features
- If for presentation, use of special syntax and other features
- Citations / References
- Items for display / demonstration
- For only submission, for publication in Proceedings or also, for presentation
- Following the style / procedures set by the particular conference
- Not forgetting the organizers (know something about them beforehand)

3. CHECKLIST FOR REVISION / EDITING

3.1 Checking for accuracy of facts and scientific text; illustrations, caption or labels; tables and charts and other graphics
- with reference tools
- with sources (primary or secondary?)
- acknowledgement of sources, accurately

3.2 Correct and consistent spelling, punctuation

3.3 Reviewing
-- Layout, design, page make-up, etc.

3.4 Browsing the Internet / Websites *(while writing for journals or conferences, to remain up to date)*

4. REFERENCING / CITATIONS

- Harvard style (author, date)
  - Frist citation in the text
  - Also at the end of the Article
  - Reference list or Bibliography (in alphabetical order or date of origin, last dates first)
- Chicago style / APA / MLA style
  - Both in-text citations and a reference list
  - In-text citations are placed within sentences and paras (e. g. Ahmed, 2014)
  - Numerical system of footnotes or end-notes with a biblio
  - In-text numbering to the corresponding number in the footnotes or end-notes
    - Citation number in superscript to the write of commas and full stop and to the left of colons and semi-colons
- House style or University or Organization style
  - Example : Numbering // 1 – 9 in numerical; 10 - .. In words

5. QUALITY CONTROL

- **Quality Assurance Reference Tools**

These are to be handy by the side of an Editor and / or Quality Controller:

- Dictionaries; PC with internet connection; some source / reference books, journals and other professional documents
- Two or more standard reference books (see slide …) on Editing / Copyediting

6. BASIC PARTS OF A PUBLICATION / BOOK

- Cover page: Title / Author / Spine
- Title page: Title / Author (with brief affiliation) / Publisher / City and Year of publication
- Inner title page or Verso or Copyright page:
  - Any notice (e. g. on approval of the MS / TS / CS; copyright. Special ack, etc.) ; Printer's line, etc.
- Acknowledgement
- Foreword / Preface / Introduction
- Table of Contents / TOC (how is this prepared and organized?)
- Glossary
- Index

7. USEFUL REFERENCE WORKS

- *Chicago Manual of Style* by University of Chicago Press
- *A Manual for Writers* (of Term Papers, Theses, and Dissertations) by Kate Turabian
- *A Manual of Style and Standards: Handy Guide to Authors, Editors, Researchers and Academics* by Manzurul Islam (In press)
- *The Scientific Journal: Editorial Policies an Practices* by Lois DeBakey
- *Oxford Advanced Learner's Dictionary of Current English* by Oxford University Press (for UK English)
- *Merriam-Webster's Collegiate Dictionary* (for US English)
- *Oxford Dictionary for Writers and Editors.*

Example:2

Writing in Science and Technology

[Acknowledgement: Professor Zia Uddin Ahmed]

PURPOSE OF REPORT

- Why publish—For record keeping
- Research objective
- To present research results
- To present in a seminar/conference

ABSTRACT

- One or two sentence about the work done
- Important note on method
- Important results
- One line significance of the study

INTRODUCTION

- Introduce the topic to a general reader
- Justify why the study was considered important to undertake
- The justification may be simple but it ought to be significant, not done simply because it has not been done before.
- How it may add to new and significant knowledge
- A hint at possible conclusion that will be drawn

RESULTS

Can be presented in several sections
- Tables
- Figures
- FINDINGS
  - Nitrate is lower than maximum permissible level
  - Ammonia is higher than maximum permissible level

REFERENCES

- Different styles
- Follow the style of the journals where the article will be sent

GENERAL COMMENTS

- English
- Brevity in presentations
- Avoiding repetition
- Reviews are mostly critical
- Dampen morale of author, but think over quietly,
- Comments useful.
- Address them - better manuscript.
- Send it again somewhere else.

TITLE

Example : 2

LEVELS OF REACTIVE NITROGEN IN SURFACE AND GROUND WATER SAMPLES OBTAINED FROM DIFFERENT PARTS OF BANGLADESH

- Sharp
- Focused
- Short
- Clear

AUTHORS AND AFFILIATION
- — Authors' name in a certain order
- — Name of the institution where the work has been carried out
- — Corresponding author

9.3 Profile / Biographical Sketch of the Compiler / Author

Manzurul Islam
PhD (Communication / Scholarly Publishing), MA (English),
PG Diploma (Journalism & Communication)

Chairman / Chief Consultant
Center for Development through Open Learning, Publishing and Communication (CEDOLPC), Dhaka

Formerly,
Vice Chancellor, ZH Sikder University of Science & Technology, Shariatpur

Adviser / Professor
Training, International Affairs, Research and Publication, and Head, Center for Open and Virtual Learning (COViL) Southeast University, Dhaka

Adviser (Professor)
Publishing, Printing, Editing, and Quality Control
Bangladesh Open University, Gazipur

Consultant
Commonwealth of Learning (COL), Vancouver, Canada
Visiting Faculty and Independent Researcher and Editor in Canada

Faculty / Senior Editor
Academic Publishing Department (English)
King Saud University, Riyadh, Saudi Arabia

Senior Researcher / Quality Controller and Publishing Specialist
Information Systems and Publications
King Abdulaziz City for Science & Technology (KACST), Riyadh

Managing Director / Editor-in-Chief
Bangladesh Books International Limited (BBI), Dhaka and National Representative of UNESCO Publications (Paris) in Dhaka

Country Chief for Bangladesh / Editor *in Dhaka*
Oxford University Press (UK)

Senior Officer *(Talks and Commentaries, English)*
External Services (for UK and SE Asia) of Radio Pakistan, Karachi Ministry of Information and Broadcasting, Government of Pakistan

Member
Bangladesh Civil Service (Administration) [for a brief period]

Lecturer / Senior Lecturer *[for a brief period]*
Department of English, in two colleges of Dhaka

- *PhD in Communication (Scholarly Publishing & Editing), USA*
- *MA in English Language & Literature, University of Dhaka (DU)*
- *Postgraduate Diploma in Journalism & Communication (DU)*
- *Advanced training in UK, USA, and Canada:*
- Oxford University, England; Stanford University, California; Simon Fraser University, British Columbia, Canada

[For general studies upto Masters level, attended Nawabpur Government High School, Notre Dame College, and Dhaka University – all in Dhaka]

Attended international conferences *in 15 countries, presenting Papers in most of those.*

Visited 41 countries *in Asia, Europe, North America, Latin America, Africa, Australia and New Zealand, some being official, academic and professional trips, others being for mere tourism.*

Authored *nineteen books and monographs (in English and Bangla), four more (in English and Bangla) are awaiting publication.*

Edited or Co-edited or supervised *publication of over 450 books, monographs, journal issues in Bangladesh and abroad.*

Published *over 130 Articles and Write-ups in Journals, Magazines and Newspapers --- a few being in international journals and publications.*

==

Currently: *(i) Carrying out research, study and writing works and (ii) running a small, independent research, training, publication and educational consultancy center from Dhaka, presently focusing on Faculty Development programs in the universities through training in Research and Publication works.*

Interests: Open, Virtual and Distance Learning; Publishing; Communication; Education and Literacy; Higher Education; Quality Assurance; Faculty Development and Capacity Building; Human Resources; Studies on South Asia; Community Development; Women Empowerment.

(iii) Visiting places of touristic or academic interest within the country and abroad, and relaxing

(iv) Re-visiting and reviving old contacts (after over 25 years' living outside the country) home and abroad and sharing ideas and experiences with members of the new generation.

(v) Browsing the internet, newspapers and magazines; watching TV programs; enjoying drama, music and cultural events; reading books; reminiscing about the past seventy years, writing memoirs.

(vi) Languages: Bangla, English, Urdu, Hindi, Arabic, German.

(vi) ***Planning for projects on***: (a) A concise, practical bi-lingual Dictionary (one each for English-Bangla and Bangla-English); (b) Publishing and editing a bi-annual Journal: *The Scholar;* (c) Establishing a modest Trust and Center for Young Scholars and Researchers at Uttara, Dhaka and / or an Endowment for Research & Publication at a university or learned society; (d) Running a regular Stipend Program for needy and meritorious students, and a small (e) Adult Literacy Center and Sustainable Self-Income Generating Vocational Center for Women & Youth in a rural area in Shariatpur, in memory of late parents.

(vii) **Academic and professional visits** were made by the Author to nearly 40 **universities outside Bangladesh** during the last 48 years since mid-sixties:

UK: Universities of Oxford, Cambridge, and London.
USA: Universities of Stanford, Harvard, Chicago, Carnegie-Mellon, George Washington, Seattle, State University of New York, Columbia, Hawai, and MIT.
Canada: Simon Fraser U, Universities of British Columbia, Victoria, Manitoba, Toronto, and Ottawa.
France: Paris-Sorbonne University
Greece: Aristotelian University, Thessaloniki
Japan: University of Tokyo, and UN University.

Singapore: Singapore National University.

Malaysia: University of Malay, and Open University of Malaysia.

Egypt: Al Azhar University, and University of Cairo.

Saudi Arabia: All eight universities of the time (1982 – 2005) in the Kingdom.

Pakistan: Universities of Karachi, Sindh, Punjab, Islamabad, and Peshawar

India: Universities of Calcutta, Biswabharati, and Madras, and Indira Gandhi National Open University   at New Delhi.

Thailand: Asian Institute of Technology.

Australia and **New Zealand:** The University of Sydney, and University of Ottago.

West Indies: University of the West Indies.

PART TWO

SOME THOUGHTS ON RESEARCH, EDUCATION AND TRAINING IN PUBLISHING

Context: BANGLADESH, SOUTH ASIA AND SIMILAR NON-ENGLISH SPEAKING REGIONS

PART TWO Contents

Dedicated to the serious, national and regional publishing professionals, academics and researchers on Publishing, policy makers and international organizations concerned with book and publishing development activities.

Section 1

Preface to Part 2:
Some Personal Reflections on the
Status of Publishing in Bangladesh

The Articles in Part 2 contained in this compilation are a few of those that were written for some national and regional newspapers and journals some years ago. Repetition of ideas and expressions is not unlikely as these were prepared at different times for a common goal – to alert the concerned agencies, both governmental and non-governmental, about a positive role they should play to improve the status of publishing in Bangladesh. The Articles appear here as they were published, sometimes with minor adaptation here and there. Their thorough revision from the original form could have made the study a separate work, not a compilation of already published Articles which went out of print now.

It is felt that despite slight repetitions, every Article attempts at touching upon some novel aspects and at bringing to light new information.

Throughout, two common themes have surfaced: First, Publishing and book trade need full-time professionals who should be suitably qualified after proper training and education. Second, Publishing should be treated as an industry by the developing countries so that their governments could consider extending maximum facilities for its infrastructure build-up, together with a qualitative growth.

It will appear, in the case of the first ten years of Bangladesh, grievances were ventilated for and on behalf of the book trade or of the publishing world (of which this Author was an active and leading member for over a decade till he had left for abroad for about quarter of a century). Problems discussed and commented upon in the Articles were later found almost similar in the developing countries. Some typical problems, exclusively critical of the Bangladesh situation, were often created by economic and political constraints.

It is hoped that the present work will encourage more elaborate, problem-solving research works or studies by enthusiasts and practitioners ultimately to improve the fate of a vitally important sector like Publishing in Bangladesh as well as in other countries of the Third World. Failure to this will only deter developments as a whole, and in intellectual and cultural spheres in particular.

Presented here also are a few selected write-ups, mainly in the form of brief reports that were published in some national and regional newspapers and journals. This may be treated as part of historical development in the publishing scenario in a young country like Bangladesh which aims to achieve middle-income status by 2021, that is within 50 years of its independence. As an update, this may not appear too high an ambition when, in early 2015, the country has been able to publish as many as 3700 new titles during its 'publishing month' (February) of the year. Despite rather difficult time due to political confusion preceding and during the month-long Ekushe Boi Mela (the annual book fair held in February for special remembrance of the martyrs of language movement of 1952) which is the biggest event of its kind in the country and for the longest duration anywhere, the figure is 20 % higher than the same time the previous year. Quality-wise, however, there may be some questions; this is where all our efforts are to be made and this is why the present book re-stresses on training and education in Publishing.

The 'reports' cover topics related to Publishing or book development activities in Bangladesh and are concerned with those, from a few, with which the present Author was deeply involved. In matters of planning and execution of the small-scale attempts referred in the reports and initiated primarily from the private, non-governmental sector, the present Author had to contribute too -- whether it was a Book Week, a Seminar, a Training Course or Workshop, or an International Book Fair. Some comments and suggestions made in these are also supplemented and corroborated by the Author in the earlier chapters of this book.

Together, the Articles and reports are expected to contribute to the understanding of the book world situation in the new, developing country. The same may be true of other countries in the developing regions.

The Articles in general are expected to draw international attention direct and thus, with external collaboration, may help remove some of the existing problems faced by the book world and finally to encourage a stable, advanced publishing activity, academically and professionally.

Academic Publishing:
Its Role and Development in
Less Advanced Regions

The article outlines the state of academic publishing in the Middle East in general, and in Saudi Arabia in particular. It includes both book and journal publication. Impediments like limited training for editors and production managers and minimum funding for marketing are discussed. It is suggested that the industry in the Middle East and other developing regions would benefit from the establishment of training programs in publishing and editing and in arranging collaborative production and co-publication ventures with those in other Asian and Western presses.

The Publishing Scene at a Glance in Some Areas in the Middle East

Books

Over the years, and especially in the recent past, publishing has had to adopt new technology to cope with the growing demand for quick and high-quality production. New publishing technology is still in its formative phase in the Middle East as in other developing regions. End users are now more quality-conscious, and they want publications faster. These requirements could be addressed by implementing modern techniques in typesetting, layout, and design, a fact that has been noticed with importance in many countries of Asia, like those in the developed world. The developing countries have also started embracing these new approaches to

135

publishing, although not in a very visible way. For example, now computerized composition is practiced, even via local networking, by the universities and research organizations, thus making it redundant to re-typeset the full text and avoiding much of the proofreading work too.

Typesetting is performed at source by the author or by the sponsoring organization; publishers only update the minimum changes and corrections, once the copy is revised by the author after proper editorial review. Publishers or organizations in the non-English speaking countries publish in English mostly for students at an advanced level, or for research or official use. Occasionally, a few reference and trade books are published by learned societies, universities or professional bodies as well as by limited private publishers. The disciplines they cover range from arts and history to botany and zoology, from pure research works in the social sciences to applied aspects of medicine and engineering. A growing number of new scholarly titles are now published almost every year. Various government departments often come out with periodically published high-quality works from the point of view of both scholarship and production.

Journals

As far as journals are concerned, one may not judge easily the scope and quality of these publications, as some of them have proven to be outstanding while others lack in a standard. Refereed journals are published quite frequently, although a predictable schedule of publication is not common enough. While specially oriented narrow disciplines are rare, mixed disciplines in combined journals are common. Universities and research centers publish specialized journals and other research publications.

Marketing

Unfortunately, only a very few commercial publishers and no scholarly publishers have taken serious steps to promote, market, and distribute their publications effectively. Private publishers send out sample copies to potential customers, display their products at exhibitions and meetings, and sell their publications with discounts, varying from 20 to 30 per cent at fairs and exhibitions. Sometimes the response to the books at exhibitions has been enormous.

On the other hand, because of lack of proper promotion, whatever is published is less known to most of the potential users, thus creating a huge vacuum. Clearly, dissemination of knowledge, culture, and information -- the main purpose of publishing -- is hampered, and authors feel discouraged when the concerned readership is not made aware of their publications or of the results of their research.

As for the journals, for wider promotion, considerable number of these need to be covered in the international indexing and abstracting services, including in journals and databases.

Marketing practices in publishing, in the modern sense, are often absent in the Middle East region. Joint efforts could be initiated to make use of the present-day facilities of the electronic media, such as through creating websites for recent and forthcoming titles. A consortium of publishers could consider, for example, regular updating of their catalogs of titles through the website. Also, on demand publications can be initiated for certain scholarly and educational titles so that large single print runs can be avoided, saving storage and related expenses. Cooperative measures or joint ventures within some sub regions (for example: South Asia, South East Asia, the Middle East) within Asia, or even globally could be convenient and feasible when medium-size or small publishers may not be able to post their marketing announcements and activities, including accepting orders online.

More attention must also be given to promote reading. Whether the subject is books or periodicals, a lack of interest in reading as a whole is observed. School and university courses must be designed to tempt students to read supplementary or recommended books, as well as some other literary or general works. Mere access to the Internet, which is still limited only to a part of the learners specially in the metropolitan areas, cannot replace reading of printed books and journals. Publishers may need to develop innovative marketing techniques for print publications, by offering special discounts, more frequently organizing book displays and fairs, announcing awards and other incentives, encouraging the greater use of libraries, making the new titles available to potential readers immediately on publication, and so on.

Editorial and Production

Many avoidable errors creep into a large number of published materials. Since most book and journal manuscripts require exhaustive editing in all aspects, only highly qualified and well-trained editors can handle the staggering problem adequately. Similarly, the contributions of skilled technical editors and copy editors cannot be ignored. The role of editors in making a manuscript worthy of publication is felt to be greater in the developing region, where the art of writing and the practice of preparing a complete manuscript -- whether general, educational, or scholarly -- are yet to be developed. Barring a few exceptions, mere peer review of the articles in academic journals, often advising authors to revise and rewrite, is not enough. However, with the help of desktop publishing, some scholars and experienced authors have started making headway in creating works by themselves in better quality than before.

In the areas of production, design, layout and quality printing, some success has been achieved. A few seasoned hands are available, although not enough; it is these professionals that manage to produce publications of good quality. Desktop publishing and other new technology are also playing a prominent role in easing the situation.

Why Publishing is Important

The encouraging fact is that the number of students pursuing post-secondary education is increasing by leaps and bounds, research is expanding, and literacy is improving at a phenomenal rate. The economies of the developing region are in better shape than those that existed a few years ago.

For these reasons, publishing as a discipline and as an occupation, an area neglected so far, has to be addressed afresh. Better quality and more numerous scholarly and educational publications must be produced. For example, during these days of modern publishing, co-publication programs, even in English, could be searched for and then implemented. Without promoting scholarship and culture through more and more publications and their proper marketing, overall development in the true sense will be missed. The developing world, with an ever-growing educated population, may see another renaissance in these fields and in the knowledge industry by undertaking steps towards encouraging full-scale publishing enterprise.

Training and Education in Publishing

To give effect to all the above, among other measures, a group of people suitably qualified and trained has to take the lead. Publishing houses still do not have facilities for in-house training. Universities and vocational or technical schools have not yet started any worthy program.

Some detailed curriculum plans and designs for various courses on publishing have been prepared by a number of publishing professionals and academics (Minowa, 2000; McGowan, 1996; Lorimer, 1990; Montagnes, 1989; Islam, 1989; Tebbel, 1984; Geiser, 1983). These educators have also analyzed publishing education in several parts of the world, clearly showing the extent of areas that could be covered by many schools of publishing.

The present author's elaboration on the matter (Islam, 1994) has the following to include: A survey conducted some years ago (which can greatly be considered relevant even today) revealed that out of 39 universities, research organizations, and other institutions of higher learning and training centers studied (not all-inclusive) in a single country, 26 published 38 journals and over 120 other publications of a scholarly or scientific nature over the preceding few years. Regarding higher education and training in publishing, such as at the graduate level, 60.47 per cent considered them desirable, and of the remaining respondents, 4.65 percent did not think they were necessary or desirable. Of the last group, 37.21 percent stressed that such programs not only are unfeasible now, but will remain so in the near future.

The persons interviewed or contacted in the survey include top university administrators, senior government officials, senior academics, and publishing professionals. Just in course of a few years, now more than 70 universities in USA and UK alone offer graduate level courses on Publishing. [A short list compiled by this Author is available at chapter ....in the present book].

Relevant to these findings, at least one university of one country in cooperation with other universities, research organizations, and ministries, hosted a national symposium on academic publishing in as early as 2001, which included a few international speakers from developed countries. Also, a national research project on developing scientific and scholarly publishing, initiated by the present author in collaboration with some more senior academics and publishing professionals, was conducted.

The availability of wide-ranging courses in a few countries (such as the United States, the United Kingdom, Australia, Canada, Japan, South Korea, China and India) signifies the need to introduce systematic education in publishing for the developing regions. It is heartening to note that just in course of a few years, now more than 70 universities of USA and UK alone offer graduate level courses on Publishing. [A short list compiled by this author is appended at the end of this article].

The sooner our policymakers and concerned agencies realize the importance of formal training and education in publishing as in all other applied disciplines, the better it will be for overall development anywhere.

Specific Action: Cooperation and Collaboration

Some developing countries in Asia and other regions have rightly had to switch over to vernacular publishing in general. Yet whatever remains there for publication in English is worth several million dollars in terms of business. To target that market, a properly planned co-publication program, along with collaboration on other publishing areas, could be attempted. Such an initiative should keep in view these primary objectives:

1. Areas of publication: Such programs could be by way of joint authorship or by way of selecting subjects of common interest, for example: religious books, children's books, or academic or research works. Common textbooks at the tertiary or advanced level or in medicine, engineering, or computer science could also be considered.

2. Areas of production: Cooperative programs might be organized around typesetting, designing, and printing those publications basically in English, that might prove expensive or complicated to the non-English speaking countries. A similar joint program may also be considered for publications that might have a small or medium –sized readership. Such initiatives like those in India, Singapore and the Philippines would avoid the high cost of production that otherwise would have to be carried out in the expensive West (Islam, 1989). Cheaper editions of essential mass market titles -- educational or trade – could also be tried, like those of McGraw Hill from India or some dictionaries from the Philippines.

3. Areas of business interest: Collaborative publishing programs could involve marketing strategies that might ease the distribution of certain publications in the various regions within Asia or even beyond; for instance, those of interest to the Middle Eastern or West Asian countries, South and South East Asia or of those to the Far East. Some trade publications could be planned for all of Asia: Heritage titles, fiction and other literary works of eminent authors, non-fiction subjects such as regional politics and economics, dictionaries, travel guides, and so on. A part of the income accruing from these projects could be diverted to more and more academic publications in which profits may be minimum, or not at all.

4. The common note. Collaborative publishing ventures would help readers learn more about Asia from Asians first, and then by others outside Asia. The focus or approach of Western authors may not serve the tastes and perception of the Asians in the best way. This market has long been the exclusive domain of the Western countries, barring a small share to India, Pakistan, Lebanon, Syria, and Egypt.

A Note of Hope and Caution

While we may stress a stronger independent approach to publishing in some areas of South Asia and elsewhere in Asia, we cannot ignore the support of the West in publishing. For instance, in addition to books on English Language Teaching (ELT) and English as a Second Language (ESL), we would require scores of other books to cover otherwise inaccessible fruits of knowledge and scholarship. No part of the developing world can afford to remain isolated from the intellectual pursuits anywhere and reflected through the print media in the advanced world. For obvious reasons, it is believed that some of the affluent countries in Asia will have to depend on British and American dictionaries, encyclopedias, and other reference books for quite a long time. Internet versions are no substitutes for all.

It is a pity that at times, simply for cultural and socio-political reasons, some valuable publications from the West cannot reach potential seekers of knowledge in the East. We should not be overly enthusiastic about discarding publishing aid from the West altogether. Instead, we should rather make necessary adaptations to the core materials or rewrite basic invaluable texts, fulfilling special rights obligations to the copyright holders. Such attempts will make suitable works available to our readers. For the very important works in English published in the West, our consortia in Asia can work more seriously on how, when, and where in the region or sub - region those could be adapted or translated.

Conclusion

The exchange of technique and other resources should help boost cooperation among the Asian and Western nations. Some countries could extend technical know-how, others marketing and distribution expertise. Such an approach, among others, would go a long way towards developing academic publishing in the less advanced regions.

The scope for reactivating and modernizing the publishing industry through future training and education is much greater in Asia than in the West. Traditional publishing is destined to continue in the greater part of Asia for quite some time, at least until it is complemented (not replaced) in a bigger way by electronic publishing which will require more capital and technology - both considerably lacking here. Providing training in publishing and editing at universities and in technical works at the vocational centers will be one step forward in the process.

Till such facilities are available at hand, education and trainings could also be received at publishing centers outside the developing region which could contribute enormously towards equipping the future human resources needs in the promising publishing sector of the region. It is hoped that further studies on publishing in general and academic publishing in particular will lead us to accept the challenges of today and the publishing opportunities of tomorrow in the developing areas in the new context.

Acknowledgement: Author's (MI) Article in *The Journal of Scholarly Publishing*, 32, No.1

References

Minowa, Shigeo (2000). *Introduction to Publishing Studies* (Tokyo: Scientific Societies Press).

Islam, Manzurul (1994). "Scholarly Publishing in Developing Countries: The Role of Publishing Education Today for Development in the Next century." Paper presented at *the 5th International Conference on Scholarly Publishing*, 6-10 May. Aristotle University, Thessaloniki, Greece.

Lorimer, Rowland (1990). "Planning a Master's Program in Publishing," *Book Research Quarterly* 6, No. 1 (Spring): pp 38-47.

Montagnes, Ian (1989). "Training Editors in the Third World," *Journal of Scholarly Publishing* 20, No. 3 (April): pp 162-172.

Geiser, Elizabeth A. (1983). "Education for Publishing", *Journal of Scholarly Publishing,* 14, No. 3 (April): pp 275-287.

Section 3

Education and Training in Publishing and Academic Publishing: Towards Self-reliance by the Developing Regions

Abstract

Of late, universities and research organizations have started realizing afresh the significance of scientific and scholarly publications, involving books, journals, reports, conference proceeding, etc. With the re-emphasized national policies in the developing regions, and in keeping pace with this age of specialization and professionalism, proper planning and required training in publishing and editing have become all the more necessary. When training publishing professionals would thus be available around, faculty members, researchers and authors would be in a better position to spend more of their time and energy in finding, creating and writing materials, rather than in simultaneous overseeing of the publishing process through.

The paper explores if the professionals in publishing can be in the making within a reasonable time. Various measures are suggested, including education in publishing at different levels, from vocational or technical to certificate or undergraduate or diploma to graduate levels; and training for the working personnel at entry level, mid-level and top management or advance level. Publishing is no more an 'accidental profession', but it is one that must adopt new techniques and technology in a systematic and scientific manner. The paper cites some examples of how and where education and training in publishing is offered in other countries. Based on his experience in the profession for over four decades, including some years with a reputed international academic publishing house (Oxford University Press), the author presents a model course in publishing, for local adaptation as well as for consideration by other developing countries.

It is concluded that with the availability of formal education and training in publishing on a national or regional basis, not only will the dependence on the academics be minimized, but also it will pave the way for standardizing academic publishing, to the benefit of all concerned -- academics, authors, editors and users.

Introduction

Education in publishing is almost absent in this part of the world. It is still in the form of only on-the-job experience, or at best in the irregular offer of some basic training and apprenticeship. The concept has changed since the mid-fifties of the last century. In today's age of specialization and professionalism, there can be education and there can be training in every field. Training is included in education as education is not excluded from training. These two terms are synonymous. Those who wish to proceed systematically, through courses of studies over a period of time during their academic career, can look for education in publishing. Others not bestowed with the advantage of receiving such schooling, may master the skill by undergoing training in different phases.

In some situations, training is preferred to formal education. At other places, education is more recommended. In regions like our own, where the very practice of publishing in general and academic or scientific publishing in particular is not that active in the modern sense and hence importance given is not enough, *education is more needed*. In this region, as in many developing countries in other regions, publishing is yet to be realized as no more 'an accidental profession' and academic publishing is yet to be considered as one of such significance that will lead the scholars and academics 'to publish or perish'. Here, publishing is commonly understood as an ordinary profession requiring sometimes simple editing, without going deep into the manuscript or 'original' (as it is known in some places), or just checking of printing errors or caring for some formatting and design, etc. This last aspect of design and look is so much so that in some affluent societies, many otherwise insignificant publications have come out in the best of glossy formats, colorful and expensive designs, whereas many significant publications have drawn minimum attention, resulting in their poor editing and production. The area of promotion and distribution requires thorough modernization to help disseminate properly all those 'products' created after strenuous effort by the authors or academics themselves.

It is in these areas, to minimize the drawbacks, that due attention is needed in publishing, and more so in academic publishing. In fact, more importance is to be paid to academic or scientific publishing, as the world outside ours is fast advancing. To keep pace with developments in the 'knowledge industry', we have to be more alert and active. For that, one of the most desired ways would be to see as soon as possible, that we can disseminate fruits of our knowledge and research or creations nationally, regionally or globally, through that still very effective medium -- publication.

Perhaps in the sciences and research works, for sharing and spreading the results and other creations, the most effective medium may soon be via electronic publishing. But that too is least likely to eliminate publishing in the print media. A trend can be noticed from Table 1 which shows that during the last couple of years especially when e-publishing has been growing, the number of traditionally published books has constantly been on the increase, too.

See Section 3.1

In the case of journals, where peer reviewing is considered an important factor, and where compliance of reviewers' comments or observations by the authors is given due weightage, conventional publishing may not perish in the near future. Peer reviewing process, if this exists anywhere, in online publications is by and large short of the desired reliability.

Thus from all counts, we need professionals and well trained manpower in the academic publishing sector where publications of original research and quality matter most, where the products or the books and journals must meet certain standards towards international acceptance.

Such human resource is far short of the need. In a first-ever seminar on academic and scientific publishing organized and held some years ago, in a leading and 60-year old university of a publishing-shy country, hardly twenty people showed interest. Only two years later, in the first-ever symposium on academic publishing, which was three-day long, preceded by an all day long two-day workshop, more than 110 publishing, writing and editing enthusiasts took part. This speaks for itself about the role and need for creating a pool of publishing professionals and specialists in areas where the field is least explored.

That is why training and education in publishing or, education and training in publishing should begin in the less advanced regions, without further delay in a planned and serious manner.

To the proponents of training-only in Publishing, without formal education in this discipline, we would like to propose: In places where Internship or hands-on training or established publishing houses having training facilities and guided supervision and making those available to non-employees or guests are very limited, the other alternative is to offer regular educational or academic courses in the universities and institutions. Without such arrangements, development of properly skilled manpower in publishing would be difficult and would take much time. Similar formal and institutional education has been around for long in other professional and technical fields, where too, on-the-job training and experience were considered the only means. For example, in recent years there has been the existence of undergraduate and graduate courses in many universities in such professional fields as: Journalism and Communication, Library and Information Science, Education, Law, Pharmacy, Computer Science, etc. Once upon a time, there used to be strong opposition to formal courses in these also.

A quick glance at the list of topics in Tables (2.1, 2.2 and 2.3) will show how detailed education in Publishing could be and why a systematic planning of the suitable curriculum is required. These are just a few of the courses that could be introduced in our universities if we were to train and educate our future workforce in this profession. Also, if we wish to establish Publishing as a respectable and important academic profession to serve the ever-increasing academic and scientific community, locally and globally, one of the principal steps would be to encourage Publishing Education—the sooner the better. The list of some institutions around the world as indicated in the Appendix will show already available publishing education programs at various levels. We should expect that similar, not necessarily the same, education in publishing will start in the developing regions like Bangladesh and other South Asian countries in the near future. Only that way our universities would consider undertaking a pioneering role, by making all concerned understand the significant role scientific and academic publishing could play towards promotion of science and scholarship.

- **3.1: Proposed topics for the courses at undergraduate and graduate levels, in Publishing Science or Publishing and Editing:**

3.1.1   FOR UNDERGRADUATE COURSES (B.S.)

- Introduction to Publishing
- Copy preparation
- Proof reading
- Layout and design
- Estimating, costing and pricing
- Graphics /Tables/ Illustrations, etc.

- Sales planning and management / sales budget / online sales / telemarketing
- Promotion, publicity, advertisement, direct mails, representatives, online promotion
- Distribution: Wholesale, retail, stock movement and control
- Trade channel: Bookshops, libraries, book clubs, exports, trade terms
- Market research and market development
- Computer application in the book trade / Internet use

- Acquisition editing / sponsoring and commissioning
- Contract drafting
- Royalties / Fees / Honorariums
- Copyrights / Subsidiary rights

- Editing: Language skill
- Grammar and composition: Rules, practices
- General editing: Publishing-type wise / subject-wise
- Journals editing

- Style of writing and common standards
- House style: Creativity and respect for universal practices
- Editor's liberty and limitations

3.1.2 FOR GRADUATE COURSES (Masters degree / Doctoral studies)

- History and concept of Publishing Science / Publishing Studies
- Publishing in the different economic and cultural contexts
- Research methodology
- Academic and Scientific writing and editing / Referencing and Citations
- Varieties of Publishing / Specialization

- Advance techniques in Publishing
- Publishing and new technology
- Research, training and development in Publishing / Publishing development

---

- Electronic and Online publishing / Internet use in Publishing
- Seminars, Symposia, Conferences
- Thesis or Dissertation
- Internship / Teaching or Research Assistantship

- Publishing management
- Economics of Publishing
- Financial management, Administration and Human Resources
- Logistics / Inventory control
- Agreement / Rights / Legal issues

3.2 Example of courses in a Masters program in Publishing introduced some two decades ago (at the Canadian Center for Publishing Studies), Simon Fraser University, Vancouver

Academic

- Communications media: Research and Development
- Text and Context
- The history of Publishing
- Technology of the Evolving form of Publishing

Professional

Publishing Law
- Theory and Practice in Writing and Editing
- Design and Production
- Marketing for the Publishing Industry
- Organizational Finance and Administration for the Publishing Industry
- Directed Studies
- Contemporary Issues Seminar
- Publishing Internship

Academic Publishing: Its Need and Role

Higher education and research activities in our part of the enlightened world have increased manifold. Publications are still found to be among the most popular and effective media in the dissemination of academic research, learning and scientific information. As such, a re-emphasized effort has become necessary in the developing countries where academic publishing has much to achieve. By itself, Publishing is now a specialized discipline and technical field.

All universities, most research organizations, some Ministries and major establishments have to handle some form of academic or research publication—books, journals, conference proceedings, research reports, etc. To publish those in high standard, or even in acceptable quality, we need well trained personnel -- Authors, Reviewers, Editors and other publishing professionals. At the same time, we would like to become self-reliant.

We are determined to improve our standards, streamline our procedures, train our people working in this specialty, and ultimately make our products (books, journals, etc.) more presentable, cost-effective and of high quality. On a review of the state of affairs in academic publishing in particular, we will see in this paper how much important it is today and, then how to develop it further.

In most less advanced countries, as well as in many advanced countries, it has been realized that even during this electronic publishing age, the significance of conventional academic publishing in the transfer of knowledge continues (Table 1).

Categories of Academic Publishing

These can be identified from any of the following:
- Scholarly publishing
- Scientific publishing
- Learned publishing
- Research publishing
- University press publishing

With slight variation, each of these categories would cover Academic Publishing too and vice versa. In one way or the other, all these terminologies overlap each other, thus creating a wide range of Academic Publishing.

For instance, supplementary books and some original books following advance university courses of study or even textbooks for advanced level would pass for Academic Publishing. Especially those in Arts and Humanities, containing well researched elaborate notes/footnotes, etc. would merit as academic publications. Some scientific journals by the academics may be termed academic publishing. Scientific or research publishing (especially if the contributions are mostly from outside the academia, that is, from the scientific and research organizations), may also be considered academic publishing. Similarly, research studies, particularly in the arts, humanities and social sciences, etc., could be termed scholarly publishing or learned publishing or research publishing, as well as academic publishing.

Academic publishing, translation and adaptation

In the context of non-English speaking countries, publications could be either original or translated or adapted. Till date, most works of advanced nature, particularly in the sciences, have been published in English. Original authorship in such areas is still minimum in other languages. Hence the quickest way to have adequate number of publications would be to select from world knowledge and to check if those would be suitable as textbooks, and then to go ahead for their translation.

If neither original works can be authored in sufficient number and in high quality, nor if translation can be arranged or if mere translation of the text as it is in the original is not considered appropriate for our target students and learners, the alternative could be to adapt the original to the need of our beneficiaries. At times this would necessitate inclusions and exclusions (of course with the permission of the copyright holders) and then, if required, minor changes or simplifications.

Not all chapters or topics may be of interest to our requirements (curriculum-wise, culturally or otherwise); selected part or greater part of the original may be used or adapted, to make it more appropriate, economic and less time-consuming. Such adaptations may not please the original author or publisher, but after the acknowledgement and fulfillment of other obligations, such changes in the translated or adapted version could enable our students to understand the text and context better and could help the original Author read by these students, not fully though. Otherwise, such Authors would remain unread and unknown in the non-English speaking world.

As indicated earlier, to prioritize our Writing, Translation and Adaptation, we have to apply our rationale for the national need, towards spread of knowledge and scholarship. There have to be practical ways of academic collaboration in publishing between advanced countries and the emerging regions. Well-trained Editors with strong background in general education in consultation with subject specialists, can make proper selection and acquisition of appropriate manuscripts for writing, translation and adaptation. In academic publishing, this natural or global cooperation is to be sought by the developing world.

Academic Publishing can play its role tremendously in coping with the progress of science and scholarship, as far as communication through publications is concerned. Adaptation has not found its way much in the developing countries. So far it has been straightway translation only. It may be viewed as a complementary method of acquisition of more and more suitable manuscripts for translation into national language. Publishing all kinds of knowledge in translation and adaptation in the absence of sufficient original works by the nationals may be worth consideration to meet part of the great need. In today's globalization, our countries need to have the fruits of knowledge from other parts of the world. In turn, those countries could benefit (i) by way of promotion of their Authors and scholarship in our regions and, (ii) if royalties, fees or whatever are the copyright obligations, are paid as required, by way of their income from abroad. The Authors and Publishers of those countries would find a better scope for the spread of knowledge and business.

To join all countries in the pursuit of knowledge and hence to contribute to the intellectual and cultural development of the fast progressing world, the increasingly important sector of publishing can no longer be left alone. A thorough survey is required to find out the exact publishing data on some developing countries, whatever the number of publications – books and journals – to promote reading and publishing.

Human Resources in Publishing Sector

Whether it is in researching and writing the results, or in selection and acquisition of suitable manuscripts or in copy preparation and editing, or in effective design of the product, or in promotion and distribution (since any publication looses its significance and the Author or the academic looses his interest, unless the potential readers or users can have it at all desired locations immediately after publication), skilled people would be required. Thus publication of journals and books has to be considered an important activity by itself, as it is also to be so for service to the academic and scientific community. Publishing needs to be treated as a modern and academic profession, which must be handled jointly by academics, and publishing professionals. For instance, in addition to writing, reviewing and evaluating the manuscripts to be published, many academics are often found struggling and wasting their otherwise valuable time in such technical or publishing areas as editing, copy-editing, proof-reading and coordination with the typesetter or compositor, designer and printer.

Self-publishing is another option (which is discussed elsewhere in this book,). Academics and scientists could, instead, devote their time and energy more fruitfully to other aspects of the search, creation and writing of the original material, rather than in the activities of the publishing process. This in itself is time consuming and technical – which should be properly cared for by the publishing professionals. In the recent past, however, Authors themselves have begun (as part of self-publishing or desktop publishing) typing out their own works, leaving little work for the Publisher's compositor, typesetter or designer.

When the need for writing, editing and typesetting is so great, academics and publishing professionals must leave much of the last two works for the professionals. To carry out this, publishing activities in the various public and private sectors like universities, research organizations, ministries and other government agencies, non-government organizations, and even self-publishing individual Authors will call for a large and adequately trained manpower.

Some obstacles

All these put together are not sufficient to meet the growing need for academic publishing or any publishing. The need is there. But there is the obvious dearth of proper Writers, Authors, Editors and of course technically trained publishing manpower. There is also the unfortunate communication gap, or lack of desired cooperation between Authors, Reviewers, Editors and Publishers or sponsors. Often there is a wide difference between what is required of Authors by various journals and academic publications in conformity with their house style and those actually practised by the contributing Authors and their own affiliated institutions.

All such pitfalls can be minimized much, if not removed in full, if professionalism in publishing and authorship grows. This should start with Academic Publishing, as most of the participants in this activity are highly qualified and capable of adopting to standards and procedures only if they become a bit more serious and if they follow the guidelines mentioned in the style sheets of the concerned publishing agencies.

Whether in following the respective procedures of individual publishing houses, or in seeing their publications in time and in an acceptable quality, it becomes the joint responsibility of all stakeholders – Authors, Reviewers, Editors, Copy-editors and press technicians.

It is well known that particularly in the academic parlor, an organization builds up its image, internally or externally, by fulfilling many objectives among which an important one being through publications. A standard publication by a reputed institution of any academic may lead him to maximum heights in terms of his recognition in the field and in his being accepted outside his own domain. In his personal career, too, by way of promotion, recognition and offer of growing responsibility, good publications by him count considerably. And a trained Publisher can contribute much in this behalf.

If highly specialized fields like computer and information science, telecommunications, medicine and engineering -- to name but a few of the many other applied professions –could be gradually tackled by the aspiring professionals from the less advanced regions, the area of publishing and printing and later a few branches of academic and scientific publishing could also be operated by them. Only requirement is the strong will, supported by, among other needs, methodical training and education in the publishing sector.

Already, several activities (Table 3) have been identified by the present Author (Islam, 2004) that could be handled satisfactorily by the new, trained professionals in a quality which could be matched with that of the advanced regions. Some could consider Publishing a career compatible with other prestigious and well-remunerative professions. Even as interns or trainee–professionals, they could take up the workload of the senior or experienced professionals to the extent of 25 – 30% at present and of 50% or more within a few years.

Checking of the tasks mentioned in the 3.3 takes much time of the technical editor or professional editor. With some training and practice, qualified new professionals can carry out these initially. After practising in these areas for a while, they will get used to other sub-editorial works, ultimately understanding more complicated editorial and production supervision works.

3.3. Sample checklist for editorial and production sections of a publishing department

1. **Originals / manuscripts:** Original copy of the manuscript (ms), and not in photocopy, plus the CD or pen drive or any digital version should be received by the publishing unit.--- Manuscript (and disk or digital format) to follow the guidelines meant for authors / typesetters; the softcopy must match the hardcopy in full

2. **Title page:**

   – Title of the book / the journal article
   – Full name(s) of the author(s)
   – Affiliation of author(s), without abbreviation
   – Postal or e-mail address of the author / principal author (if more than one)

3. **In journal articles:** Are the section headings, sub-headings, etc. in their proper order?

4. **References:** Are these in proper sequence and order, following house style? Make sure that the sources mentioned in the reference list correspond with those cited in the text, according to the system followed consistently?

5. **Illustrations / Tables / Graphics:** Are they properly labeled, with necessary legends, captions, serial numbers, etc. An additional copy (photocopy) of each figure, plate, map is to be provided.

6. **Pagination:** Serial numbering of the complete manuscript (before pagination is made automatic), including figures, tables, attachments, etc. is to be written in pencil (or erasable ink) first.

    –   In the proof, do the pages have proper running heads (for both even and odd pages, with author, title) and serial auto numbering?

Training in the other important areas of Publishing, that is, in actual editorial works which have more to do with the intellectual aspect, would depend on the quality of general education that each Editor will bring along as his background, as well as on his subsequent determination to master this skill. If a number of new professionals could work for some editorial specialties in many newspapers and periodicals, well qualified academics could consider devoting their time and ability in academic and scientific editorial works, with the objective of making this a career, with compatible facilities and incentives. The above observation has been made based on a survey, in a particular year, of the various works involved in over 100 publications – journals and academic books -- and on close follow-up of routine works of over twenty publishing professionals and more than 200 authors, reviewers and specialized editorial board members and their assistants.

Also the checklist at 3.3 above will supplement this study.

Of interest can be 3.1, indicating part of traditional publishing activities globally (this is without reference to journals and periodicals). The volume of activity being carried out in traditional publishing even today in this fast growing electronic publishing era only rules out the current perception of the too ambitious electronic publishers who see paperless publishing replacing the former in the near future. A visit to the annually held international Frankfurt Book Fair which has been there annually for sixty-six years, and the ever-increasing number of new titles every year will continue to encourage authors and conventional publishers worldwide. Although the situation might affect much the journals sector everywhere, books and monographs shall continue to be dominated by the paper copy publishing at least in our developing countries for a long time. This offers more scope for education and training of publishing professionals in the existing practices.

Conclusion

It is concluded that publishing is viewed as the *sine qua non* of all academic endeavor because it is through publishing that academics mainly communicate the results of their scholarly pursuits and systematic enquiries to the universe. Therefore, unless such skill is developed in favor of academic publishing, scholars attempting to communicate their research across disciplines may find that the information transmitted by them after meticulous research is not always the one received by the target audience. A sound and suitable publication system is the answer. To implement that, qualified skilled manpower would be required and to develop that badly needed human resource, properly planned education and training in publishing would be essential.

Table: Showing number of published titles (books) per year in some countries of the world

Country	25 years ago(1990)	15-17 years ago (1998-1999)	Recent (2011-2014)
USA	46,743	64,711	304,912
UK	63,756	100,700	184,000
Canada	14,231	18,573	19,900
Germany	61,015	77,889	82,048
Russian Federation	28,716	45,026	101,981
France	38,414	47,214	41,902
Malaysia	3,320	5,816	17,923
Japan	40,576	65,438	82,589
South Korea	21,000	27,313	47,589
India	55,000	57,386	90,000
Australia	6,676	6,835	28,234
USA	46,743	64,711	304,912
UK	63,756	100,700	184,000
Canada	14,231	18,573	19,900
Germany	61,015	77,889	82,048
Russian Federation	28,716	45,026	101,981
France	38,414	47,214	41,902
Malaysia	3,320	5,816	17,923
Japan	40,576	65,438	82,589
South Korea	21,000	27,313	47,589
India	55,000	57,386	90,000
Australia	6,676	6,835	28,234

Source: International Publishers Association, Geneva, 2014

Acknowledgement: Author's (MI) *Paper presented at the 5th International Conference on Scholarly Publishing*, Aristotle University, Thessaloniki, Greece.

References

Minowa, Shigeo (2000). *Introduction to Publishing Studies* (Tokyo: Scientific Societies Press).

McGowan, Ian (1996). "Publishing Education Worldwide: A Scottish Perspective in a Newish Art", *Logos* 7, No. 2: pp 19, 168-174.

Islam, Manzurul (1994). "Scholarly Publishing in Developing Countries: The Role of Publishing Education Today for Development in the Next century." Paper presented at *the 5th International Conference on Scholarly Publishing*, 6-10 May. Aristotle University, Thessaloniki, Greece.

Lorimer, Rowland (1990). "Planning a Master's Program in Publishing," *Book Research Quarterly* 6, No. 1 (Spring): pp 38-47.

Montagnes, Ian (1989). "Training Editors in the Third World," *Journal of Scholarly Publishing* 20, No. 3 (April): pp 162-172.

Islam, Manzurul (1989). "Research and Scientific Publishing in Saudi Arabia", *International Library Review, London,* 21: pp 355-361.

Tebbel, John (1984). "Education for Publishing," *Literary Trends* (Fall).

Geiser, Elizabeth A. (1983). "Education for Publishing", *Journal of Scholarly Publishing,* 14, No. 3 (April): pp 275-287.

Section 4

Publishing Development in South Asia: A Bibliographic Overview

Publishing has long been neglected as an important activity in comparison with other components of the communication technology. This disregard is more conspicuous in the developing countries. Publishing should have had a wider role as it also contributes significantly towards national development in the cultural, economic, intellectual, scientific and technical spheres.

While tremendous growth of the printed word is noticed in the advanced countries, despite the competitive impact of electronic media there, nothing spectacular has been achieved in Bangladesh or in South Asia, with the exception of India, or in other developing countries.

One of the principal factors is the lack of desired communication internationally on the advancement of academic, scientific and technological pursuits in the region. Whatever has been achieved, has not found proper dissemination beyond borders. This gap will only widen if along with other media, research activities are not advanced with the active aid of suitable publications.

Publishing being so important in etching an international image for the region's scholarship and learning, as well as for expanding research activities which also aim at permanence through quality publications, advancement of publishing must be attempted methodically.

One major way to do this could be by treating publishing as a science and technology and to proceed accordingly. On its very perception as a scientific and technological discipline, its systematic and serious study will grow. Publishing could be regarded, among other actions, as a full academic discipline for Graduate and advanced studies in some select universities of the region. A regional Publishing Development and Research Institute (as has been presented in a separate chapter in Part II of this volume) could also be established to acquaint and train the practitioners with advance ideas and latest techniques of modern publishing. More and more incentives could be generated to grow publishing as a commerce and industry too. National development and priority functions could include book development and related activities, along with publishing development and research.

To serve as a feedback for such education and training as well as to support professionals and researchers alike, some reference literature will be needed. A select bibliography on Publishing is expected to meet this demand to some extent.

Although, some bibliographies have been prepared on the related areas, such as on Asia or on the Third World, no specific study of the kind has been made on Bangladesh and South Asia in particular. One such work, *Book publishing: A Select Bibliography on Bangladesh and South Asia* by the present author is a brief and exclusive treatment towards that end. More comprehensive investigations should be carried out by other enthusiasts and researchers. Before long, detailed bibliographies should be made available to all concerned.

The need for such reference tool on publishing is likely to be felt in greater intensity with the development of systematic regional cooperation in matters of education, science and culture, and particularly after the emergence of such bodies as SAARC,

South Asian Association for Regional Cooperation, which has Bangladesh, Pakistan, India, Sri Lanka, Nepal, Bhutan, Maldives and now also Afghanistan as members. Over the years, the current author has had the opportunity of knowing firsthand, the state and development of publishing in the region, also having visited all the member countries of the region and having worked in at least three of these countries.

On following the recommendations presented in the study, the South Asian region could create incentives and examples for other regions or separately for countries with more similarities to one another. The group could as well serve as an indicator for further development in publishing in the rest for the Third World, in Asia, Africa and Latin America.

In previewing bibliography, it has been repeatedly felt that there is no alarming dearth of literature on Publishing as is generally feared by the involved persons. In fact, and surprisingly enough, more literature on some developing countries and regions is available abroad than those that are found within a particular country or region itself. For instance, one rather rare field of Publishing on which much has been written abroad is Scholarly Publishing, although not enough has been covered on the developing countries.

Reasons for rapid growth on the literature on Scholarly Publishing are attributed to the regular publication of a few international journals since early seventies of the twentieth century. *Journal of Scholarly Publishing* from the University of Toronto Press has remained the principal contributor in this role. Also, a significant role has been played by the occasional inclusion of topics on Publishing in the other related journals and periodicals, like *Library Trends* from Illinois, *Unesco Journal of Information Science, Librarianship and Archives Administration* (now defunct) from Paris, *Publishers Weekly* from New York, *The Bookseller* from London,

The Indian Book Industry from New Delhi, *The Book Development* from Tokyo and *The UNESCO Newsletter* (now defunct) from Karachi. The sources are further enriched by contribution of papers presented in several conferences and seminars, sponsored particularly by such bodies as Association of American University Presses, Society of Scholarly Publishers, Association of Scholarly Publishers in South East Asia, American Publishers Association, Publishers Association of Great Britain, Federation of Indian Publishers and Booksellers Associations, International Federation of Scientific Editors Associations and similar others.

In Bangladesh, however, some articles and papers have been published on the local situation in Publishing. The periodicals like *'Boi'* (The Book), *'Boier Khobor'* (The Book News), and the national newspapers including leading weeklies publish articles from time to time. Not more than two books have been published in the last ten years on publishing itself, although not exceeding a dozen have been published in the international arena either.

The same applies to studies on publishing in general in other South Asian countries. Articles are published sporadically in the trade journals like *"Grontho Jagat"* from Kolkata and *"The Indian Book Industry"* from New Delhi. Some more are published from Karachi in the *Newsletter* of the UNESCO Regional Office for Book Development and Culture in Asia and the Pacific. A number of papers are presented by officials and professionals alike in meetings and conferences held in South East Asia, as well as in the Far East. Articles published and papers presented in the national languages of South Asian countries were contributed by local publishing professionals while those in English were authored by local and foreign experts, journalists and academics.

Compared to allied professions, such as journalism, library and information science, literature on publishing is indeed meager.

Therefore, for suitable and sufficient studies on publishing in general, some specific and vigorous programs should be undertaken like those once attempted in connection with the preparation of *"Books About Books"* by different agencies. All such references could serve well the purpose of further research and advance studies or academic courses on publishing even at Graduate level.

One Bibliography by the present Author containing 158 entries, made an attempt to provide relevant reference materials on publishing in particular, keeping in mind introduction of a future academic course, at the level of Graduate studies in select universities in South Asia. Special attention has been paid to Bangladesh, Pakistan and India – the three countries comparatively more active in publishing than the others in the region.

As is the case in any bibliography, the one under review does not claim to be all-comprehensive. Sources incorporated were those that could be reached after study of some similar standard works, together with the present compiler's own investigation including his personal visit to the concerned agencies in most countries of the region and through his online search from national and international data bases. These searches did not exclude lapses and omissions.

It would be a worthwhile effort to make a study of the available bibliographies themselves like Altbach and Rathgeber's or UNESCO Karachi's, and other relevant literature on books and publishing. This could be achieved also by making a fresh search on the subject in all appropriate data bases, libraries and information centers, book fairs and then by preparing a master compilation on Publishing. Altbach and Rathgeber have made a stupendous attempt, but that too contains a part, significant though, of all that is available around the world, and not enough from Bangladesh and South Asia. Perhaps some agencies like the UNESCO, with active support of individual compilers in the field, and of national organizations, could refurbish such a broad-based bibliography on publishing in the region.

In the bibliography under review, although some old references are included prior to the seventies, special coverage is for a short period which is the eighties in particular and the seventies in general. One on the later years must be prepared before it is out of date too.

For both the Preface and the Overview discussed in this review, the Author has freely used contents from one of his research projects, *"Advancement of Publishing as a Science and Technology in the Developing Countries: A Study of Scholarly Presses".*

Section 5

A Proposal for a Regional Institute of Book and Publishing Development and Research / *Context: South Asia*

1. BACKGROUND

1.1 Aims and Objectives

As a follow-up of one proposal presented some years ago by this Author to the SAARC Secretariat in Kathmundu, the issue is raised here once again for the establishment of a Regional Institute of Book and Publishing Development and Research (RIBPDR). Before and since then some countries have either set up or upgraded their national bodies like National Book Development Councils (NBDC) or Centers (NBC), some other countries have not yet been able to follow suit.

After further study and experience, particularly after having conducted some research in recent times, the present Author is convinced of a new, integrated approach: To cope with the fast developments made in the information arena and other related technologically advanced fields, publishing development should be undertaken more explicitly, side by side with book development. To match growing and changed demands of the twenty-first century where paper copies or published literature will be weighed, perhaps from a different perspective, with more chances of being 'devalued', mere book development as a cultural concern may not be adequate. Development of a full-fledged industry, as well as a reinvigorated commerce, will be more needed in the form of concerted effort towards survival of the book.

1.2 The Need: Why a Regional Institute?

Specially in the developing countries where resources in skilled manpower, suitable infrastructure and required finance are limited, such joint or collaborative initiatives will be most required. By any single country (except one or two) among, say, the eight South Asian nations or among some more in South East Asia, it may not be feasible for the lack of the above support, to run two separate organizations for book and publishing development. Also to avoid overlapping, a centralized regional organization, in addition to the national ones (discussed elsewhere in this volume) with active involvement in publishing and book development may be set up soon. Therefore, and to further improve the status and quality of book and publishing activities as well as to maintain greater cooperation, a regional institute (in cooperation with the national agencies like Councils or Centers) may be established simultaneously as an integrated approach. This Institute will combine the major components of the book – writing, editing, production and distribution.

The organizational structure, function and operation of the proposed Institute are briefly outlined in the three Tables (at the end of this chapter). Although some similarities of the functions will be noticed, these will rather re-emphasize the need for having an exclusive Institute of Book and Publishing Development and Research at regional level. Such an Institute will also help the governments formulate suitable plans to standardize publishing and book development, which would contribute to educational, cultural and informational as well as economic or industrial sectors. The Institute will help create required infrastructure and environment and will provide research programs of both pure and applied nature. These steps would ultimately contribute to the attainment of high level of efficiency and standard in the field.

Book and publishing professionals would grow both quantitatively and qualitatively. Like any other research and development organization, the Institute will publish the research results; prepare guideline and standards and when necessary will also offer consultation services to both private and public sectors. Efforts to establish co-operation and to maintain coordination among the various agencies in the region -- institutions and publishing establishments -- will be included in the Institute's concerns. Holding of seminars, workshops, conferences; awarding prizes; recognizing services of talented publishers, model institutes and standard commercial publishing houses in the region in a befitting manner will be added to the Institute's priority activities. With such performances, the routine works like exchange of information, initiation of training, and regular program will be undertaken

1.3 Research Potentialities and Development of Publishing

A glance at the following, as mere suggestions, will show how involved an Institute might be towards research and development potentialities alone, unlike the present book development organizations.

It is feared that in the days to come, the book is likely to be 'the danger of becoming the ultimate casualty' in dissemination of information and knowledge. Research is needed to analyze the concepts, elaborate the problems confronting publishing industry and suggest new measures to overcome the critical situation.

Aims of such steps should be to prove that 'traditional book is an extra-ordinary convenient and inexpensive artifact (even at today's prices); we do not believe it will become obsolete'.

Comprehensive research will be needed to find out the extent to which adoption of new technology in information may eliminate books or their mode of production and distribution. Conversely, thorough research may help indicate how information and communication technology could improve and speed up production, reduce price and boost sales of publications and hence contribute to development of publishing.

Research should also lead to the development of further indigenous publishing, based on new technology, and should suggest how developing regions like Bangladesh or South Asia could aim at minimizing imports and at expanding exports of publications.

Further research will be required to measure the impact of an integrated effort in developing publishing through education, training, and advance studies. The joint role and cooperation must be investigated to see how far the practitioner-publishers and the academic faculty could contribute in educating and training not only the publishing and book professionals but also all those who are involved in writing, editing, producing, distributing, reading, or in any aspect of the publication process.

It is evident that among a few active tools, serious research on some critical issues of publishing and the book should be conducted to establish the growth of publishing. In this behalf an independent Institute like the proposed one is expected to play a significant role.

2. ORGANIZATION OF RIBPDR

General outlines of a proposed Regional Institute of Book and Publishing Development and Research (RIBPDR) are presented here for consideration by the authorities. The same structure with necessary amendments could also be applied for adaptation by a similar organization at the national level by other countries in the region. A case as an example is the establishment of the SAARC University in New Delhi which, however, is unique and has larger agenda to fulfill. Institutions like the one proposed by us here (RIBPDR) would also be another example of regional cooperation. At the same time, development of a vital field like Publishing through training and education need be executed without further delay.

2.1 *Membership*

2.1.1   **Core Membership** in the RIBPDR will be open to all government organizations, allied agencies, institutions and individuals with obligation to collaborate with the Institute for its smooth functioning and growth.

2.1.2   **Supporting Membership** will be offered to organizations and individuals, both in the private and public sectors, who will contribute substantial financial assistance to the development of the Institute's programs.

2.2 *Management*

The RIBPDR shall have a Board of Governors or a Governing Body (G.B) and an Executive Council (E.C). The latter will function under the general policies and guidelines to be framed by the former and will be the full-time agency to run the affairs of the Institute.

All members of the G.B. (except the Ex-officio member who will be the Executive Director or Chief Executive Officer of the Institute), including the Chairman and the Vice Chairmen, will be nominated/elected for a two-year term. Full meetings of the G.B. will be held annually or bi-annually. These sessions will review policies, financial standing and major programs. The G.B. will also appoint the Executive Director or the CEO.

The G.B. will be constituted thus, with 13 or more members (see Table 1):

2.2.1 *Board of Governors*
Chairman / Vice Chairmen (1+2)

Chairman: An eminent, respectable and senior litterateur or educationist or scholar of acceptable standing or the Minister in charge of Cultural Affairs or Education or Science & Technology of any member country.

Vice Chairmen: (i) The Secretary to the concerned Ministry (for instance, Cultural Affairs, Education, or Science and Technology) of a member country, and (ii) an eminent educationist or scholar or litterateur will be the two Vice Chairmen.

Members: (10) A: *From officials (3):* Three senior government officials from three different member countries will form this membership. These officials will be drawn from individuals of or above the rank of Joint Secretaries to the government of the different departments or divisions of the member countries. They will preferably represent ministries concerned in one way or the other with book and publishing development or research or planning or industry or commerce.

> B: *From Professionals (3):* Three members from among eminent educationists / academics / scholars; readers / librarians; authors / writers; designers / publishers / printers or booksellers / binders, etc.

> C: *From Supporting Members (3):* Three members from those individuals who will have made substantial financial contribution to RIBPDR for its development and for some of its specific programs.

D: *Secretary or Chief Co-coordinator* (1): This person will be an Ex-officio member and will be the Executive Director (or Director General or Chief Executive Officer of the Institute, whatever is the title). He will also be the Chairman of RIBPDR's Executive Council.

In this 13-member Board of Governors (the number of which may be increased or decreased depending on the size of total membership), representation should be from as many departments, organizations, professions as possible. No particular professional group will have more than one-third representation on the Board. The book and publishing related personalities directly involved may have up to half of the total representation in specific sub-committees if desired expertise or resources are not available at hand.

The ex-officio member, being the Executive Director of RIBPDR, will be a non-voting member of the G.B. The non-voting member will be entitled to full participation in the G.B. meetings; his expert opinions and recommendations will be given due consideration by the voting members in final decision on every policy issue and major program.

Voting rights for members will be valid for those who will have met their financial (if any) and other obligations to RIBPDR before the annual or bi-annual G.B. meetings.

2.2.2 *Executive Council*

This Council, to be headed by the Executive Director or CEO of RIBPDR, and to comprise all Heads of Divisions of the Institute, will be responsible for the execution of all policies and decisions taken by the G.B. It will monitor steps taken for the fulfillment of the aims and objectives of the Institute. It will also plan and develop new programs and review the already undertaken ones. The Council will be the management body of the Institute for all activities and operations within the guidelines framed by the Board.

For vital decisions or changes, senior appointments, major programs, the Executive Director will work in consultation with the Council.

The Executive Council will recommend the annual budget to the G.B. for approval and will suggest measures to maintain or develop the financial standing of the Institute. (See Table 2 for more details).

2.3 *Operations*

2.3.1 **Personnel**

For routine, day-to-day operations of the Institute, the Executive Director and the senior members of the staff of RIBPDR like Heads of Divisions or Departments or Programs will be responsible. They will be assisted by a required number of professional, technical and support staff (See Table 3 for details).

Emoluments, benefits and terms of service of the staff shall be commensurate with similar regional institutes or organizations.

2.3.2 **The Executive Director**

The ED of the Institute will be a strong professional /expert in the field of book or publishing activities and in related research.

The Executive Director will be supported by 4-5 senior professionals, each able to handle and develop specific programs independently, working in close coordination with other departments and divisions.

2.3.3 Operation Facilities

The Institute will be provided with necessary research and training facilities. It will also have model showroom-cum-library or information center containing a select list of indigenous publications as well as publications on book and publishing related topics on or of interest to the country and the region. Such list will include Reference literature on books and training by the Institute.

3. PROGRAMS

3.1 Regular Programs

Suitable programs will be initiated and undertaken specially in the following areas: Book development; publishing development; liaison and coordination of similar offices and organizations; research in the Institute itself and coordination of applied research in the field by other agencies; conduct of training; seminars, workshops and symposia; publication of in-house materials and reference works for the trade; and dissemination of information on the Institute and its activities. See Table-3.

3.2 Other Programs

From time to time the Institute may draw up income generating programs (such as consultation services, etc.) which will not compete with those carried out by its sister national organizations or by the indigenous publishing industry of a member country.

4. INCENTIVES AND AWARDS

The Institute will introduce several awards and programs as incentives to all concerned towards development of RIBPDR. Among such awards and incentives, the following are proposed for initiation:

4.1 RIBPDR Fellowship
4.2 RIBPDR Chartered Membership
4.3 RIBPDR Alumni/Participant Membership
4.4 RIBPDR Grants for Applied Research

4.1 IBPDR Fellowship

4.1.1 **Resident Fellowship**

To those who will undertake on-campus or resident research/study/ teaching for a fixed period from 3 months to 1 year (extendable in rare cases) on any aspect of book and publishing development activity approved by the Institute.

4.1.2 **Visiting Fellowship**

To those extraordinary individuals (i) who will make presentation of their lifelong expertise or experience in arranged seminars/ workshops; (ii) will share the fruits of the same with the Faculty and senior students/trainees of the Institute for a short period (say, 8 to 10 weeks), and (iii) will present the outcome in the form of a standard publication (monograph, report, book, etc.) from the Institute.

4.1.3 **Honorary Fellowship**

To those eminent and talented individuals who will have demonstrated exemplary contribution to any aspect of book and publishing activity and who may be considered useful or supportive in the promotion of the Institute's programs, aims and objectives.

4.2 Chartered Membership

4.2.1 *Chartered Membership*

This will be conferred on those founding applicant individuals, institutions, publishing houses or book development agencies, (a) having achieved desired standards and success in book or publishing activities; (b) believing in the aims, objectives and development of the Institute itself; (c) are prepared to work for the promotion of the Institute.

4.2.2 *Chartered Associate Membership*

Will be for those founding members in the allied professions like printing, binding, paper manufacturing, bookselling, librarianship, information science, journalism, education, business administration, or as authors, scholars, educationists or academics, or as artists and designers.

Such members will be expected to work for the promotion of book and publishing development, remaining in their respective professions.

4.2.3 *Chartered and Associate Chartered Membership*

This will be conferred only on those individuals or applications in categories stated here earlier and shall be either by nomination or by examination or interview. Awardees will be expected to have attained highest professional standards in publishing or book development activities in their community or country by themselves or by special courses at the Institute or by its sponsored agencies. Both will be required to keep up the image and prestige of the Institute.

4.3 Alumni/Participant Membership

This will be open to any student, alumni or trainee or participant in any course or program of the Institute. Such a potential member will be proposed for membership by any Faculty / Division/ Department of the Institute or by another Member or Fellow of the Institute.

4.4 Grants for Applied Research

4.4.1 *Granting Research Awards*

Grants will be awarded by the Institute to support and monitor applied research in book and publishing in the region. Priorities will be given to researches, results of which are likely to be utilized in the local context and without much financial burden on the implementing agencies.

This would be extended by inviting research proposals from talented individuals and active organizations.

4.4.2 *Other Research*

Basic research will also be conducted in the Institute itself to facilitate applied and other researches.

In addition, whenever it will be feasible, the Institute will undertake research projects sponsored by international and other agencies and will offer its consultation services to governmental or corporate bodies.

4.5 Other Awards and Scholarships

Occasionally, other awards and graduate student scholarships initiated by the Institute itself or to be proposed by any other organization will be introduced also.

5. A PROJECT OFFICE – THE START

Once the objectives and the need for the proposed Institute are accepted in principle, financial and other necessary requirements could be studied for feasibility and early implementation. A project could be set up immediately to work out details and give shape to the Institute within a short time.

A project office for the proposed RIBPDR could be established on a two-to-three year commissioning, initially with the financial and technical support of a few founding members.

6. CONCLUSION

The role of organizations like the UNESCO can be great in the first phase, for study, coordination and initial functioning of the project office. At a later stage, UNESCO could organize and offer consultation services and liaise international cooperation.
Some objectives of the proposed Institute may apparently seem overlapping with some of the existing UNESCO offices such as the National Book Center. But on close scrutiny it would be observed that the Institute will primarily be engaged in research,

development, advance training and graduate studies in book and publishing science.

Presently most activities in the current national center cover book promotion aspects, and short, irregular and temporary trainings. Also included in such centers are cultural activities. These are often akin to slow public sector ventures usually restrained by official or bureaucratic procedures with stress on coordination works, routine reporting and surveys. On the other hand, the Institute will function like an independent or autonomous university of small size, with a wide scope for research and consultation activities leading to development as well as for training the middle and top level professionals for the future. These will include training the trainers, and identification, encouragement, affiliation or recognition to individuals and establishments in both book and publishing related fields.

Table-1.

RIBPDR Board of Governors

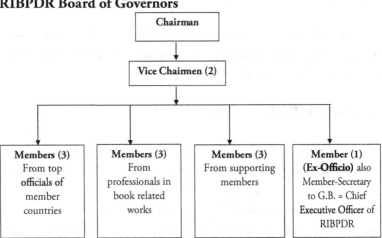

Chairman

Vice Chairmen (2)

Members (3) From top officials of member countries	Members (3) From professionals in book related works	Members (3) From supporting members	Member (1) (Ex-Officio) also Member-Secretary to G.B. = Chief Executive Officer of RIBPDR

Table-2

Executive Council and Organizational Chart of the Proposed Regional Institute of Book and Publishing Development and Research (RIBPDR)

1) *Chairman*
Chairman's Functions
Advisers

1. Meetings of G.B.
2. Execution of G.B. policies
3. Management and development of RIBPDR
4. Directory supervision of the principal programs
5. Liaison with the host country's government, national and international organizations.

= Chief Executive Officer of RIBPDR
= Executive Director (or Director General) of RIBPDR. (Status/rank = Joint Secretary or above to the Ministry/government; or Professor of a University, with relevant expertise and interest).

= 2 from Governing Board (G.B.) + 3 experts to be nominated by Chairman, Executive Council (E.C.)

2) *Secretary*
Secretary's Functions

1. Meetings of E.C.
2. Personnel and Finance affairs
3. Assistance to Chief Executive Officer/DG/ED of RIBPDR
4. Liaison with the governments of the Member countries for finance, administration, and other cooperation as decided by the E.C.

= Secretary or Head of Administration of RIBPDR. (Status/rank = Deputy Secretary to Ministry of any government; or Associate Professor of a University.

3) Head, Book Development, RIBPI   **4) Head, Publishing Developme RIBPDR**   **5) Head, Research/Training/Publication and Information, RIBPDR**   (6-9)**

(Programs)   **(Programs)**   **(Programs)**

Center for Book Development	Center for Publishing Development	Center for Research, Training, Publication, and Information

(6-8) 3 Representatives from Advisers to G.B , specially for legal, financial and technical affairs (at least one should be from Supporting Members).
(9) One Representative (by rotation) from among the similar national organizations/committees.

Note: **G.B.** = Governing Board/Board of Governors. **Vice Chairmen** = Will assist the Chairman and shall carry out his functions in his temporary absence.
E.E. = Executive Council.

Status of **Head of Divisions/Programs** will be on individual merit, equivalent to University Professors, Associate Professors or government officials of comparable, similar national institutions.

** Three representatives from **Advisers** and one Representative from among the similar national organizations/Committees will be elected/nominated to the Executive Council for a 2-year term.

Table-3

Functional Aspects of the Programs/Divisions of the Proposed Regional Institute of Book and Publishing Development and Research (RIBPDR)

Center for Book Development (CBD)	Center for Publishing Development (CPD)	National Liaison Offices/Branches Division (NLOBD)	Center for Research, Training, Publication and Information (CRTPI)
1. Management of the unit	1. Management of the unit	1. Management of the unit	1. Management of the Unit
2. Exhibitions/Book Fairs	2. Liaison with both private and public sectors of the publishing industry in the region	2. Execution of RIBPDR programs (both book development and publishing development related)	2. Coordination of CRTPI related programs from CED and CPD.
3. Competitions/Awards		3. Coordination/Cooperation with all national organizations for common programs in the region	3. Grants by RIBPDR to NIBPDRs for applied research on book and publishing development works
4. Liaison with and feedback to CRTPI	3. Liaison with and feedback to CRTPI	4. Reports from affiliated national organizations and their review by RIBPDR	4. Seminars, symposia, conferences, meetings, workshops, etc.
5. Execution of all book development-related programs	4. Execution of all publishing development-related programs	5. Feedback to and support of Research, Training and Publication programs of NIBPDRs.	5. Research (R) and Training (T) Division
6. National showroom of selected indigenous books	5. Liaison with selected allied industries (e.g. paper, printing, binding etc.)		5.1 Research programs of RIBPDR
7. Coordination with selected model bookshops/libraries in the region	6. Regional showroom of selected indigenous journals and non-book publications		5.2 Graduate courses
8. Promotion of reading habits.			5.3 Advance professional trainings
			6. Publication (P) and Information (I) Division
			6.1 Publication & distribution of RIBPDR works:**
			6.2 Information dissemination and public relation for RIBPDR
			6.3 Reference Library for RIBPDR

** 6.1.1 Reference literature on book and publishing development
6.1.2 In-house literature
6.1.3 Technical reports, monographs, training manuals, etc.
6.1.4 Research reports of projects under Grants
6.1.5 Journals on book publishing development.

References

1. *Scholarly Communication: The Report of the National Inquiry.* Baltimore and London: The Johns Hopkins University Press. 1979. p 33.
2. Islam, Manzurul. *Book Promotion: Development in Bangladesh.* UNESCO Newsletter (Quarterly). Karachi. January, 1978.
3. Kefauver, W.A. ed. *Scholars and Their Publishers.* New York: Modern Language Association. 1977. pp. 3-5

Reference in General

Islam, Manzurul. *Advancement of Publishing as a Science and Technology in the Developing Countries: A Study of Scholarly Presses with Reference to Three Muslim Countries: Bangladesh, Pakistan, and Saudi Arabia.* Unpublished Ph.D. Dissertation. USA, 1987.

[NOTE: To treat it independently, the above proposal on the Regional Institute has been adapted in line with the one on National Institute (see Article # 6); most of the discussions being more or less the same. Concerned authorities for consideration of the Regional or the National one will review either of the two, at separate forums, for implementation. -- Author].

Section 6

Proposal for
an Institute of National Book
and Publishing Development
and Research, Bangladesh

1. BACKGROUND

1.1 Aims and Objectives

As a follow-up of one proposal presented some years ago by this author, the issue is raised here once again for the establishment of a Naional Institute of Book and Publishing Development and Research (NIBPDR). Before and since then some agencies and departments within and outside the government have either set up units or wings with a smaller scope in a different format or have upgraded a bit the existing National Book Center (NBC) by including or re-emphasizing some functions related to book development. In Bangladesh, the Biswa Shahitya Kendro, Bangla Academy, Academic and Creative Publishers Forum, Bangladesh Publishers and Booksellers Association, Library Association of Bangladesh, are but a few such bodies serving the sector that periodically care for publishing, editing, marketing, training and cooperation. Whatever they carry out, leave much room for a systematic, regular training and development program. This in turn will ultimately create a new set of young, talented, enthusiastic persons who would devote full-time to the profession. All such initiatives will take publishing to the highest levels as in some other new fields of software development, online and open learning, informatics and the like.

After some more study and experience in the past few decades, and particularly after having conducted some research in the field in recent times, the present author is convinced of a new, integrated approach for the overall development of the book and publishing as a modern field of professional, cultural and academic activity. To cope with the fast developments made in the information arena and other related technologically advanced fields, publishing development should be undertaken more explicitly, side by side with book development.

To match growing and changed demands of the twenty-first century where paper copies or published literature will be weighed, perhaps from a different perspective, with more chances of being 'devalued', mere book development as a cultural concern may not be adequate. Development of a full-fledged industry, as well as a reinvigorated commerce, will be more needed in the form of concerted effort towards survival of the book. The scope has to be expanded beyond the service of only knowledge and culture. Commercial and industrial interests at the national level, and then at the global level, will have to be the other concerns, alongside love and emotion for the book as a separate issue.

1.2 The Need: Why a National Institute?

Specially as in the developing countries, resources in skilled manpower, suitable infrastructure and required finance in Bangladesh are limited; so collaborative initiatives will be most required. It may not be feasible for the lack of the above support, to run two separate organizations for book and publishing development. Also to avoid overlapping, a centralized national organization, in addition to the ones (discussed elsewhere) already existing with active involvement in publishing and book development may be set up soon. Therefore, and to further improve the status and quality of book and publishing activities as well as to maintain greater cooperation, a regional institute (in cooperation with the national agencies like Councils or Centers) may be established simultaneously as an integrated approach. This Institute will combine the major components of the book – writing, editing, production and distribution.

The organizational structure, function and operation of the proposed Institute are briefly outlined in the three Tables. Although some similarities of the functions will be noticed, these will rather re-emphasize the need for having an exclusive Institute of Book and Publishing Development and Research at national level. Such an Institute will also help the governments formulate suitable plans to standardize publishing and book development, which would contribute to educational, cultural and informational as well as economic or industrial sectors.

The Institute will help create required infrastructure and environment and will provide research programs of both pure and applied nature. These steps would ultimately contribute to the attainment of high level of efficiency and standard in the field. Book and publishing professionals would grow both quantitatively and qualitatively. Like any other research and development organization, the Institute will publish the research results; prepare guideline and standards and when necessary will also offer consultation services to both private and public sectors.

Efforts to establish co-operation and to maintain coordination among the various agencies nationwide -- institutions and publishing establishments -- will be included in the Institute's concerns. Holding of seminars, workshops, conferences; awarding prizes; recognizing services of talented publishers, model institutes and standard commercial publishing houses in the country in a befitting manner will be added to the Institute's priority activities. With such performances, the routine works like exchange of information, initiation of training, and regular program will be undertaken.

1.3 Research Potentialities and Development of Publishing

A glance at the following, as mere suggestions, will show how involved an Institute might be towards research and development potentialities alone, unlike the present book development organizations.

It is feared that in the days to come, the book is likely to be 'the danger of becoming the ultimate casualty' in dissemination of information and knowledge. Research is needed to analyze the concepts, elaborate the problems confronting publishing industry and suggest new measures to overcome the critical situation.

Aims of such steps should be to prove that 'traditional book is an extra-ordinary convenient and inexpensive artifact (even at today's prices); we do not believe it will become obsolete'.

Comprehensive research will be needed to find out the extent to which adoption of new technology in information may eliminate books or their mode of production and distribution. Conversely, thorough research may help indicate how information and communication technology could improve and speed up production, reduce price and boost sales of publications and hence contribute to development of publishing.

Research should also lead to the development of further indigenous publishing, based on new technology, and should suggest how a developing country like Bangladesh could aim at minimizing imports and at expanding exports of publications.

Further research will be required to measure the impact of an integrated effort in developing publishing through education, training, and advance studies. The joint role and cooperation must be investigated to see how far the practitioner-publishers and the academic faculty could contribute in educating and training not only the publishing and book professionals but also all those who are involved in writing, editing, producing, distributing, reading, or in any aspect of the publication process.

It is evident that among a few active tools, serious research on some critical issues of publishing and the book should be conducted to establish the growth of publishing. In this behalf an Institute like the proposed one is expected to play a significant role.

2. ORGANIZATION OF NIBPDR

General outlines of a proposed National Institute of Book and Publishing Development and Research (NIBPDR) are presented in the Tables for consideration by the authorities. With the structure as shown here, necessary amendments could also be applied for adaptation. Development of a vital field like Publishing through training and education, is expected to be materialized by an organization like NIBPDR without further delay.

2.1 Membership
This will comprise two or more groups as the following:

2.1.1   **Core Membership** in the NIBPDR will be open to all government organizations, allied agencies, institutions and individuals with obligation to collaborate with the Institute for its smooth functioning and growth.

2.1.2   **Supporting Membership** will be offered to organizations and individuals, both in the private and public sectors, who will contribute substantial financial assistance to the development of the Institute's programs.

2.2 Management

The NIBPDR shall have a Board of Governors or a Governing Body (G.B) and an Executive Council (E.C). The latter will function under the general policies and guidelines to be framed by the former and will be the full-time agency to run the affairs of the Institute.

All members of the G.B. (except the Ex-officio member who will be the Executive Director or Chief Executive Officer of the Institute), including the Chairman and the Vice Chairmen, will be nominated/elected for a two-year term. Full meetings of the G.B. will be held annually or bi-annually. These sessions will review policies, financial position and major programs. The G.B. will also appoint the Executive Director or the CEO.

The G.B. will be constituted thus:
9 or more Members, wherever possible, by including a good representation from well-qualified female nominees.

2.2.1 Board of Governors

Chairman: An eminent, respectable and senior litterateur or educationist or scholar of acceptable standing or the Honorable Head of State (as in the case of private universities of the country, the constituted state Commissions or the National Scouts) or the Minister in charge of Cultural Affairs or Education or Science & Technology.

Vice Chairmen: An eminent and respectable educationist or scholar or litterateuer will be Vice Chairperson. Alternatively, the Secretary to the concerned Ministry (for instance, Cultural Affairs, Education, or Science and Technology), will be the Vice Chairperson.

Members (7):

A: *From Officials (2):* Three senior government officials will form this membership. These officials will be drawn from individuals of or above the rank of Joint Secretaries to the government of the different departments or divisions. They will preferably represent ministries concerned in one way or the other with book and publishing development or research or planning or industry or commerce.

B: *From Professionals (3):* Three members from among eminent educationists, academics and scholars; readers and librarians; authors and writers; designers, publishers, printers or the book trade, etc.

C: *From Supporting Members (2):* Three members from those individuals who will have made substantial financial contribution (as endowment or charity) to NIBPDR for its development and for some of its specific programs.

D: *Secretary or Chief Co-coordinator* (1): This person will be an Ex-officio member of the G.B. and will be the Executive Director (or Director General or Chief Executive Officer of the Institute, whatever is the title). He will also be the Chairman of NIBPDR's Executive Council.

In this 9-member Board of Governors (the number of which may be increased or decreased depending on the size of total membership and available Budget), representation should be from as many different departments, organizations, professions as possible. No particular professional group will have more than one-third representation on the Board. The directly book and publishing related personalities and experts may have up to half of the total representation in specific sub-committees if desired expertise among the Board Members is not available at hand.

The ex-officio member, being the Executive Director of NIBPDR, will be a non-voting member of the G.B. The non-voting member will be entitled to full participation in the G.B. meetings; his expert opinions and recommendations will be given due consideration by the voting members in final decision on every policy issue and major program.

Voting rights for members will be valid for those who will have met their financial and other obligations, if any (for example, personal presence in Meetings and Programs) to NIBPDR before the annual or bi-annual G.B. meetings.

2.2.2 *Executive Council*

This Council, to be headed by the Executive Director of NIBPDR, and to consist of all Heads of Divisions of the Institute, will be responsible for the execution of all policies and decisions taken by the G.B. It will monitor steps taken for the fulfillment of the aims and objectives of the Institute. It will also plan and develop new programs and review the already undertaken ones. The Council will be the management body of the Institute for all activities and operations within the guidelines framed by the Board.

For vital decisions or changes, senior appointments, major programs, the Executive Director will work in consultation with the Executive Council.

The Executive Council will recommend the annual budget to the G.B. for approval and will suggest measures to maintain or develop the financial standing of the Institute. (See Table 2 for more details).

2.3 **Operations**

2.3.1 *Personnel*

For routine, day-to-day operations of the Institute, the Executive Director and the senior members of the full-time staff of NIBPDR, like Heads of Divisions or Departments or Programs will be responsible. They will be assisted by a required number of professional, technical and support staff, full-time or part-time (See Table 3 for details).

Emoluments, benefits and terms of service of the staff shall be commensurate with similar national institutes.

2.3.2 ***The Executive Director*** of the Institute will be a strong professional or expert in the field of book or publishing activities and in related research as well as a committed individual with proven success in planning, management and resource sharing, preferably with international networking experience.

The Executive Director will be supported by 4-5 senior professionals, each able to handle and develop specific programs independently, working in close coordination with other departments and divisions.

2.3.3 *Operational Facilities*

The Institute will be provided with necessary research, training and funding facilities. It will also have model showroom-cum-library or information center containing a select list of indigenous publications as well as publications on book and publishing related topics on or of interest to the country. Such list will include Reference literature on books and training by the Institute. Resource sharing, e-library and internet facilities should be widely and easily accessible to all stakeholders -- users, participants, trainees, researchers, professionals and support staff.

3. Programs

3.1 *Regular Programs*

Appropriate programs will be initiated and undertaken specially in the following areas:

- Book development
- Publishing development
- Liaison and coordination with similar offices and organizations
- Research in the Institute itself and coordination of applied research in the field by other agencies
- Conducting training, seminars, workshops and symposia
- Publication of in-house materials and reference works for the profession and the trade, and

- Dissemination of information on the Institute and its activities (See Table-3).

3.2 *Other Programs*

From time to time, the Institute may draw up income generating programs (such as consultation services, trainings and workshops, publications, etc.) which will not compete with those carried out by its sister national organizations or by the indigenous or commercial publishing industry of the country.

4. Incentives and Awards

The Institute will introduce several awards and programs as incentives to all concerned towards development of NIBPDR. Among such awards and incentives, the following are proposed for initiation:

4.1 NIBPDR Fellowship
4.2 NIBPDR Chartered Membership
4.3 NIBPDR Alumni / Participant Membership
4.4 NIBPDR Grants for Applied Research

4.1 NIBPDR Fellowship

4.1.1 *Resident Fellowship*

To those who will undertake on-campus or resident research, study, teaching for a fixed period from 3 months to 1 year (extendable in rare cases) on any aspect of book and publishing development activity approved by the Institute.

4.1.2 *Visiting Fellowship*

To those extraordinary individuals (i) who will make presentation of their lifelong expertise or experience in arranged seminars or workshops or Lectures; (ii) will share the fruits of the same with the Faculty and senior students or trainees of the Institute for a short period (say, 8 to 10 weeks), and (iii) will present the outcome in the form of a standard publication (monograph, report, book, etc.) from the Institute.

4.1.3 *Honorary Fellowship*

To those eminent and talented individuals who will have demonstrated exemplary contribution to any aspect of book and publishing activity and who may be considered useful or supportive in the promotion of the Institute's programs, aims and objectives.

4.2 Chartered Membership

4.2.1 *Chartered Membership*

This will be conferred on those applicant individuals, institutions, publishing houses or book development agencies, (a) having achieved desired standards and success in book or publishing activities; (b) believing in the aims, objectives and development of the Institute itself; (c) and are preparing to work for the promotion of the Institute.

4.2.2 *Chartered Associate Membership*

Such Membership will be for those in the allied professions like printing, binding, paper manufacturing, bookselling, librarianship, information science, journalism, education, business administration, or as authors, scholars, educationists or academics, or as artists and designers.

Such members will be expected to work for the promotion of book and publishing development, remaining in their respective professions.

Both Chartered and Associate Chartered Membership will be conferred only on those individuals or applications in categories stated here earlier and shall be either by nomination or by examination or by interview. Awardees will be expected to have attained highest professional standards in publishing or book development activities in their community or country by themselves or by special courses at the Institute or by its sponsored agencies. Both will be required to keep up the image and prestige of the Institute.

4.3 Alumni or Participant Membership

This will be open to any student, alumni or trainee or participant in any course or program of the Institute. Such a potential member will be proposed for membership by any Faculty, Division, or Department of the Institute or by another Member or Fellow of the Institute.

4.4 Grants for Applied Research

4.4.1 *Granting Research Awards*

Grants will be awarded by the Institute to support and monitor applied research in book and publishing in the country. Priorities will be given to researches, results of which are likely to be utilized in the local context and without much financial burden on the implementing agencies.

This would be extended by inviting research proposals from talented individuals and active organizations.

4.4.2 *Other Research*

Basic researches will also be conducted in the Institute itself to facilitate applied and other researches.

In addition, whenever it will be feasible, the Institute will undertake research projects sponsored by international and other agencies and will offer its consultation services to governmental or corporate bodies.

4.5 Other Awards and Scholarships

Occasionally, other awards and graduate student scholarships initiated by the Institute itself or to be proposed or sponsored by any other organization will be introduced also.

5. A PROJECT OFFICE – THE START

Once the objectives and the need for the proposed Institute are accepted in principle, financial and other necessary requirements could be studied for feasibility and early implementation. A project could be set up immediately to work out details and give shape to the Institute within a short time. A Project Office for the proposed NIBPDR could be established on a two-to-three year commissioning, initially with the financial and technical support of a few founding members or by the government itself.

6. CONCLUSION

The role of organizations like the UNESCO can be very great in the first phase, for study, coordination and initial functioning of the Project Office. At a later stage, UNESCO could organize and offer consultation services and liaise international cooperation.

Some objectives of the proposed Institute may apparently seem overlapping with some of the existing UNESCO offices such as the National Book Center. But on close scrutiny it would be observed that the Institute will primarily be engaged in research, development, advance training and graduate studies in book and publishing science.

Presently most activities in the current national center cover book promotion aspects, and short, irregular and temporary trainings. Also included in such centers are cultural activities. These are often akin to slow public sector ventures usually restrained by official or bureaucratic procedures with stress on coordination works, routine reporting and surveys. On the other hand, the Institute will function like an independent or autonomous university of small size, with a wide scope for research and consultation activities leading to development as: Training the trainers, and identification, encouragement, affiliation or recognition to individuals and establishments in both book and publishing related fields.

References

1. Islam, Manzurul. "National Book and Publishing Development: A Proposal for an Institute or a Council" in *The Bookworld in Bangladesh*. Publications and Information International, Dhaka. 1987. pp 85-104.
2. *Scholarly Communication: The Report of the National Inquiry.* Baltimore and London: The Johns Hopkins University Press. 1979. p 33.
3. Ibid. "Book Promotion: Development in Bangladesh". *UNESCO Newsletter* (Quarterly). Karachi. January, 1978.
4. Kefauver, W.A. ed. *Scholars and Their Publishers.* New York: Modern Language Association. 1977. pp 3-5

Reference in General

Islam, Manzurul. *Advancement of Publishing as a Science and Technology in the Developing Countries: A Study of Scholarly Presses with Reference to Three Muslim Countries: Bangladesh, Pakistan, and Saudi Arabia.* Unpublished Ph.D. Dissertation. 1987.

[NOTE: To treat it independently, the above proposal on the National Institute has been adapted from the one on Regional Institute (see Article # 5), most of the discussions being more or less the same. Concerned authorities for consideration of the National or the Regional one may review either of the two, at separate forums, for implementation].

Table-1
NIBPDR Board of Governors

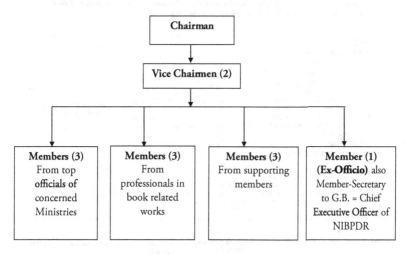

Table-2

Executive Council and Organizational Chart of the Proposed Regional Institute of Book and Publishing Development and Research (RIBPDR)

---

1) *Chairman*
Chairman's Functions
    Advisers

1. Meetings of G.B.	= Chief Executive Officer of
2. Execution of G.B. policies	RIBPDR
3. Management and development of RIBPDR	= Executive Director (or Director
4. Directory supervision of the principal	General) of RIBPDR. (Status/rank =
programs	Joint Secretary or above to the
5. Liaison with the host country's	Ministry/government; or Professor of
government, national and international	a University, with relevant expertise
organizations.	and interest).

= 2 from Governing Board (G.B.) + 3 experts to be nominated by Chairman, Executive Council (E.C.)

2) *Secretary*
Secretary's Functions

1. Meetings of E.C.	= Secretary or Head of Administration of
2. Personnel and Finance affairs	RIBPDR. (Status/rank = Deputy Secretary to
3. Assistance to Chief Executive Officer/DG/ED of RIBPDR	Ministry of any government; or Associate
4. Liaison with the governments of the Member countries for	Professor of a University.
finance, administration, and other cooperation as decided	
by the E.C.	

3) Head, Book Development, RIBPI   **4) Head, Publishing Developm(**   **5) Head, Research/Training/Publication and**   **(6-9)****
                                          RIBPDR   **Information, RIBPDR**

   (Programs)   **(Programs)**   **(Programs)**

Center for Book Development	Center for Publishing Development	Center for Research, Training, Publication, and Information

**(6-8)   3 Representatives from Advisers to G.B , specially for legal, financial and technical affairs (at least one should be from Supporting Members).
**(9)   One Representative (by rotation) from among the similar national organizations/committees.

Note: **G.B.** = Governing Board/Board of Governors. **Vice Chairmen** = Will assist the Chairman and shall carry out his functions in his temporary absence.
           E.E. = Executive Council.

        Status of **Head of Divisions/Programs** will be on individual merit, equivalent to University Professors, Associate Professors or government officials of comparable, similar national institutions.

        ** Three representatives from **Advisers** and one Representative from among the similar national organizations/Committees will be elected/nominated to the Executive Council for a 2-year term.

Table-3

Functional Aspects of the Programs/Divisions of the Proposed Regional Institute of Book and Publishing Development and Research (RIBPDR)

Center for Book Development (CBD)	Center for Publishing Development (CPD)	National Liaison Offices/Branches Division (NLOBD)	Center for Research, Training, Publication and Information (CRTPI)
1. Management of the unit	1. Management of the unit	1. Management of the unit	1. Management of the Unit
2. Exhibitions/Book Fairs	2. Liaison with both private and public sectors of the publishing industry in the region	2. Execution of RIBPDR programs (both book development and publishing development related)	2. Coordination of CRTPI related programs from CED and CPD.
3. Competitions/Awards		3. Coordination/Cooperation with all national organizations for common programs in the region	3. Grants by RIBPDR to NIBPDRs for applied research on book and publishing development works
4. Liaison with and feedback to CRTPI	3. Liaison with and feedback to CRTPI	4. Reports from affiliated national organizations and their review by RIBPDR	4. Seminars, symposia, conferences, meetings, workshops, etc.
5. Execution of all book development-related programs	4. Execution of all publishing development-related programs	5. Feedback to and support of Research, Training and Publication programs of NIBPDRs.	5. Research (R) and Training (T) Division 5.1 Research programs of RIBPDR 5.2 Graduate courses 5.3 Advance professional trainings
6. National showroom of selected indigenous books	5. Liaison with selected allied industries (e.g. paper, printing, binding etc.)		6. Publication (P) and Information (I) Division 6.1 Publication & distribution of RIBPDR works:** 6.2 Information dissemination and public relation for RIBPDR 6.3 Reference Library for RIBPDR
7. Coordination with selected model bookshops/libraries in the region	6. Regional showroom of selected indigenous journals and non-book publications		
8. Promotion of reading habits.			

** 6.1.1 Reference literature on book and publishing development
6.1.2 In-house literature
6.1.3 Technical reports, monographs, training manuals, etc.
6.1.4 Research reports of projects under Grants
6.1.5 Journals on book publishing development.

Section 7

Proposed Courses on Publishing and Editing at Undergraduate and Graduate Levels

[The following topics for the proposed Courses at undergraduate and graduate levels, in Publishing Science or Publishing and Editing, have been presented in an earlier Section in a different context; the same are repeated here for a quick reference by concerned institutions planning to introduce such Courses]:

7.1 FOR UNDERGRADUATE LEVEL (B.S.)

- Introduction to Publishing
- Copy preparation
- Proof reading
- Layout and design
- Estimating, costing and pricing
- Graphics / Tables/ Illustrations, etc.

- Sales planning and management / sales budget / online sales / telemarketing
- Promotion, publicity, advertisement, direct mails, representatives, online promotion
- Distribution: Wholesale, retail, stock movement and control
- Trade channel: Bookshops, libraries, book clubs, exports, trade terms

- Market research and market development
- Computer application in the book trade / Internet use

- Acquisition editing / sponsoring and commissioning
- Contract drafting
- Royalties / Fees / Honorariums
- Copyrights / Subsidiary rights

- Editing: Language skill
- Grammar and composition: Rules, practices
- General editing: Publishing-type wise / subject-wise
- Journals editing
- Style of writing and common standards
- House style: Creativity and respect for universal practices
- Editor's liberty and limitations

7.2 FOR GRADUATE LEVEL (Masters degree / Doctoral studies)

- History and concept of Publishing Science / Publishing Studies
- Publishing in the different economic and cultural contexts
- Research methodology
- Academic and Scientific writing and editing / Referencing and Citations
- Varieties of Publishing / Specialization
- Advance techniques in Publishing

- Publishing and new technology
- Research, training and development in Publishing / Publishing development
- Electronic and Online publishing / Internet use in Publishing

- Seminars, Symposia, Conferences
- Thesis or Dissertation
- Internship / Teaching or Research Assistantship

- Publishing management
- Economics of Publishing
- Financial management, Administration and Human Resources
- Logistics / Inventory control
- Agreement / Rights / Legal issues

Section 8

Supplement

List of universities conducting courses in Publishing and Editing at Graduate level (not all inclusive):

USA

- New York University
- Pace University, New York
- Rochester Institute of Technology, New York
- Arizona State University
- University of Denver, The Publishing Institute

[also, Stanford University, California: Advance Professional Publishing Course, since 1978 which has recently been suspended after 32 years but has been restarted at Yale University, since 2010]

CANADA

- Simon Fraser University, Vancouver [Canadian Center for Studies in Publishing] University of Toronto

[also, Banff Publishing Workshop, Alberta (since 1981), not a graduate course though.]

UK

- Loughborough University, Department of Information and Library Studies, Aberdeen
- Middlesex University, Middlesex

- University of Plymouth, Faculty of Arts and Design, Exeter
- University of Sterling, Center for Publishing Studies, Sterling
- London College of Printing Technology, London
- Oxford Brookes University, Oxford
- University of the Arts, London
- University of Leeds
- Kingston University

FRANCE

- The University of Paris XIII

NETHERLANDS

- Leiden University

ONLINE COURSES

Some Graduate courses in Publishing are also offered online by the following universities:

- The Robert Gordon University, Aberdeen
- Rosemont College, Pennsylvania
- University of Houston – Victoria, Texas
- Augsburg College, Minneapolis

MALAYSIA

- University Malaya (University of Malay), Kuala Lumpur

*Additionally, Publishing courses (long and short) are also available outside North America and Europe, in some universities and institutions in **Australia, Japan, China, South Korea, India,** etc.*

==

Section 9

Appendix

9.1 **BIBLIOGRAPHY ONE:** SOME SELECTED WORKS ON RESEARCH, EDUCATION AND TRAINING IN PUBLISHING AND ACADEMIC PUBLISHING

9.1.1 *GENERAL REFERENCE*

- *Oxford Advanced Learner's Dictionary of Current English*
- *Merriam – Webster's Collegiate Dictionary*
- *The Chicago Manual of Style.* [16th edition, 2010].
- Judith Butcher's *Copy-editing: The Cambridge Handbook*
- Kate Turabian's *A Manual for Writers of Term Papers, Theses, and Dissertations*
- *The Canadian Style: A Guide to Writing and Editing*
- Karen Judd's *Copyediting: A Practical Guide*
- *Oxford Dictionary for Writers and Editors*
- *Author Handbook: University of Columbia Press*
- *University of Minnesota: Style Manual*
- Ian Montagnes' *Editing and Publication: A Training Manual*

References on Style for Online / Website

- Janice Walker and Todd Taylor. *The Columbia Guide to Online Style.*
- Chris Barr and the Yahoo! Editorial Staff. *The Yahoo! Style Guide: The Ultimate Sourcebook for Writing, Editing and Creating Content for the Web.*

9.1.2 ***FOR SPECIFIC ACADEMIC DISCIPLINES***

a) **Humanities, Social Sciences and Sciences in general**

- *A Manual for Writers of Research Papers, Theses, and Dissertations,* 7th Edition: Chicago Style for Students and Researchers, by Kate L. Turabian. (Commonly called "Turabian style".)
- *MLA Handbook for Writers of Research Papers* by Joseph Gibaldi. (Commonly called "MLA style".)
- *Publication Manual of the American Psychological Association* by the American Psychological Association. Primarily used in social sciences. (Commonly called "APA style".)
- *AMA Manual of Style: A Guide for Authors and Editors* by the American Medical Association. Primarily used in medicine. (Commonly called "AMA style".)
- *Scientific Style and Format: The CSE Manual for Authors, Editors, and Publishers* by the Council of Science Editors. Used widely in the natural sciences, especially the life sciences. (Commonly called "CSE style".)
- *ACS Style Guide: Effective Communication of Scientific Information,* 3rd ed. (2006), edited by Anne M. Coghill and Lorrin R. Garson, and ACS Style Guide: A Manual for Authors and Editors (1997). Primarily used for the physical sciences, such as physical chemistry, physics, and related disciplines. (Commonly called "ACS style".)
- *IEEE Style: Mainly for Engineering Sciences*

b) **Business**

- *The Business Style Handbook, An A-to-Z Guide for Effective Writing on the Job,* by Helen Cunningham and Brenda Greene.
- *The Gregg Reference Manual,* by William A. Sabin.

c) **Law**

- *The Bluebook Uniform System for Citation,* developed jointly by the faculty at Harvard and Columbia Universities' Schools of Law.

d) Journalism

- *The Associated Press Stylebook*, by the Associated Press (AP).
- *The New York Times Manual of Style and Usage*, by The New York Times

Any other authentic book of reference by any reputed international publisher may also be consulted.

e) Publishing Education

Minowa, Shigeo (2000). *Introduction to Publishing Studies* (Tokyo: Scientific Societies Press).

McGowan, Ian (1996). "Publishing Education Worldwide: A Scottish Perspective in a Newish Art", *Logos* 7, No. 2: pp 19, 168-174.

Islam, Manzurul (1994). "Scholarly Publishing in Developing Countries: The Role of Publishing Education Today for Development in the Next century." Paper presented at the 5th International Conference on Scholarly Publishing, 6-10 May. Aristotle University, Thessaloniki, Greece.

Lorimer, Rowland (1990). "Planning a Master's Program in Publishing," *Book Research Quarterly*, 6, No. 1 (Spring): pp 38-47.

Islam, Manzurul (1989). "Research and Scientific Publishing in Saudi Arabia", *International Library Review, London,* 21: pp 355-361.

Montagnes, Ian (1989). "Training Editors in the Third World," *Journal of Scholarly Publishing* 20, No. 3 (April): pp 162-172.

Tebbel, John (1984). "Education for Publishing," *Literary Trends* (Fall).

Geiser, Elizabeth A. (1983). "Education for Publishing", *Journal of Scholarly Publishing,* 14, No. 3 (April): pp 275-287.

9.2 BIBLIOGRAPHY TWO: AUTHOR'S WORKS

9.2.1 Author's (MI) works related to Publishing, Editing, Quality Assurance, Open and Distance Learning (ODL)

A) On Academic and Research Writing, Editing and Publishing
From the Author's 19 published books and monographs, over 125 Articles in Journals and other periodicals, and from about 15 Papers presented in several Conferences

*[**An autobiographical note:** The following are some of the selected and published Articles, Papers or Texts that have been written by the present Author, MI, and published or presented in different works over a long period, mostly during 1987 – 2015. Major part of writings (over 12, listed here) in later years, specially during 2001- 2010, focused on Open and Distance Learning in which area the Author specifically worked; some more writings during 2011 – 2015, not included here, covered again issues on Publishing and Editing].*

1. Education and Training in Publishing: Towards Self-reliance by the Nationals (with special reference to Academic, Research and Professional Writing). *[Proceedings of The First Saudi International Symposium on Academic Publishing, sponsored by King Saud University (KSU), Riyadh, 2001]. 49 – 63.*

2. Academic Publishing and the University Presses: The Case in a Developing Region. *[Journal of Scholarly Publishing, University of Toronto Press, Canada. 32, No.1 October, 2000], 24 – 32.*

3. Publishing Education in the Developing Countries: Its Need to Modernize the Industry (Context: The Middle East and Other Asian Countries). *Paper presented at the 8th International Forum on Publishing Studies, Kuala Lumpur, 1 – 2 September,1999].*

4. Editing Science Journals in the Emerging Regions: Needs and Opportunities for Training. *[Paper presented at the 6th International Conference for Science Editors, Sharm El-Sheikh, Egypt, June, 1998].*

5. Training and Orientation Program for Saudis Wishing to Make Editing and Publishing a Career. *[Keynote presented at the first KSU Press Seminar on Academic Publishing, held at KSU Press, May, 1997].*

6. Scholarly Publishing in Developing Countries: The Role of Publishing Education Today for Development in the Next Century. *[Paper presented at the 5th International Conference on Scholarly Publishing, Aristotle University, Thessaloniki, Greece, 6 – 10 May, 1994].*

7. Research and Scientific Publishing in Saudi Arabia. *[International Library Review, London, 21, 1989], 355 – 361.*

8. Advancement of Publishing in the Developing Countries: A Study of Scholarly Presses with Special Reference to Bangladesh, Pakistan and Saudi Arabia. *[The current Author's PhD Thesis, USA, 1987].*

B) *Of relevance to Writing, Editing and Publishing*

9. *Keynote at a Workshop on Academic and Research Writing and Editing: Why and How,* North South University, Dhaka, 2014.
10. Book: *The Bookworld in Bangladesh* (with focus on Professional Editing and Publishing), Publications and Information International, Dhaka, 1989.
11. Book: *Book Publishing: A Select Bibliography on Bangladesh and South Asia,* Publications and Information International, Dhaka, 1989.
12. Report: Preface to the Author's research project, *Promotion of Science and Technology in Saudi Arabia through Publishing.* King Abdulaziz City for Science & Technology, Riyadh, 1989.
13. Journal: *The Bookman,* a quarterly journal for publishers, librarians, and researchers. Editor: MI (the present Author). Bangladesh Books International, Dhaka, 1979.
14. *Acknowledgement:* Synopsis and Salient Features from various University Teachers' Workshops on Academic and Research Writing and Publishing (designed and directed by the present Author). *[Held at Bangladesh Open University, Gazipur, 2005 - 2007; Southeast University, Dhaka, 2008 - 2010; North South University, Dhaka, 2014; Shahjalal University of Science & Technology, Sylhet, 2014; East West University, Dhaka, 2015].*
15. *Acknowledgement:* Handouts and Lecture Notes by the Author from a Course on Desktop Publishing *[at the Center for Publishing Studies, Simon Fraser University, Vancouver, Canada. 1995].*
16. *Acknowledgement:* Handouts and Lecture Notes by the Author from Stanford Publishing Course *[Advance Professional Course in Publishing at Stanford University, California, USA, 1983].*

C) *A few other publications in Bengali by the Author, covering writing, editing and publishing in general, published from Dhaka.*

17 – 22. Six Articles in the *Boi (The Book),* a monthly magazine, National Book Center, Dhaka (1970 – 1982).
23. *Songskriti'r Shebai Grontho Unnoyoner Bhumika (Role of Book Development in the Service of Culture).* An Article published in the *Boi-er Khobor (The Book News),* a quarterly magazine in Bengali, Muktodhara, Dhaka. Vol 1, No.1, 1979.

D) ***Some Articles on Publishing and Writing that appeared in various community magazines in Bengali, in Riyadh*** [where the Author worked for over two decades, during major part of 1982 - 2005].

24. From a forthcoming book on *Prokashona O' Shompadona Proshongo* (All About Publishing and Editing). Forthcoming, by a Bangladesh publisher from Dhaka.

25. A Survey of Publications in Bengali in a Place Where the Language is Different. Survey conducted in Riyadh and published in the form of a Report. Dhaka University Alumni Forum, Saudi Arabia Chapter, Riyadh, 2004.

26. "Shushthu Shompadona O' Prokashona" (in Bengali) (Standard Editing and Publishing), Article published in the community magazine, *Mohona*, Bangladesh Writers' Forum, Riyadh. 2003.

27. Book: *Shikhyadan ebong Shikhyabaybostha* (Teaching and Educational Administration) written by Khaleda Manzur, and compiled, partly co-authored and edited by Manzurul Islam (two Articles on Education, Higher Education, also with some coverage to educational publishing and editing, etc.). 2002, 2011. The Scholar, Dhaka. 116 pp.

28. Book: *Shwadhinota, Muktijuddho, Probash Jibon O' Onnyannyo* (in Bengali) (Independendence, Liberation War, Expatriate Life and Other Essays); two Articles are on Higher Education, Open Learning, etc. (also slightly covering academic publishing, editing, quality assurance, etc.). 2002, 2011. The Scholar, Dhaka. 160 pp.

E) Unpublished Thesis, Papers and Presentations:

29. Manzur's ***Theory of Three-Pronged Approach*** (to Publishing and Book Development). Developed in the Author's PhD Thesis (1987), and casually covered in various Articles and Proposals (1987 – 2004) on the subject (Publishing and Book Development).

30. Manzur's ***New Theory on Faculty Development through Research and Publication.*** Developed for the Author's presentations in various Workshops and Training Programs (2005 – 2015) designed and directed by him and sponsored mostly by the Center for Development through Open Learning, Publishing and Communication (CEDOLPC), Dhaka.

F) Some select Articles, Papers, other write-ups by the Author (MI) on Open Learning, Distance Education, most of which dealt directly or indirectly with or touched upon Education and Publishing too.

OPEN AND DISTANCE LEARNING - related expertise, works / studies

Published works

31. (2013). "Higher Education and Social Justice through Open Learning: Bangladesh Perspective". Paper accepted for presentation in the UNED-ICDE 2013 International Conference on Open and Distance Learning, held in Madrid, Spain (7-9 March). 8 pp

32. (2010). "Improving the Standard of Private Universities in Bangladesh: Some Observations" [with some discussion on Open and Distance Education]. *The Star Campus, Dhaka [24 January].*

33. (2009). "Open and Distance Learning: A Supplementary Mode of Delivery in Higher Education and Some Views on Education Policy 2009". *The Daily Star, Dhaka. [14Dec '09].*

34. (2008). "Open and Distance Learning/ICT-initiated Functional Adult Literacy for Sustainable Livelihoods: Case Study in a Pilot Project at a Remote Rural Area of Bangladesh". Paper presented at the *5th Pan-Commonwealth Forum on Open Learning*, held in London from 13 – 17 July and published in the *Proceedings.* 10 pp.

35. (2007). "Education for the Maximum through Open and Distance Learning and Quality Assurance in the Bangladesh Context". *The Bangladesh Quarterly*, Ministry of Information, Government of Bangladesh, January – March. pp 65 – 71.

36. (2006). "Contribution of One Mode of Delivery and Training Towards Capacity Building in ODL and Alleviation of Poverty through Expanded Education. Context: An Open University in South Asia (Bangladesh)". Paper presented at the Conference and published in

Proceedings of the 4th Pan Commonwealth Conference on Open Learning, held in Oct - November in Jamaica, West Indies. 8 pp.

37. (2006). "Objectives and Introductory Remarks". Address at the *BOU Teachers' Training Program on Capacity Building for Open and Distance Learning Materials*" held from 12-19 March at Bangladesh Open University, Gazipur. [Being published in the *Proceedings*. 5pp].

38. (2005). "Open Learning, Its Acceptability through Innovative Evaluation and Research in the Less Developed Countries". Paper presented at the Conference, and published in the *Proceedings of the 11th Cambridge International Conference on Open and Distance Learning*, held during 20-23 September at Cambridge University, UK. pp 81-87.

39. (2005). "Education for All, Higher Education and Training for the Maximum through Innovative Approaches: Development of Bangladesh in the New Millennium". Paper presented at a symposium held in Riyadh, Saudi Arabia by University Alumni Forum of Bangladesh (UAFB), 22 April.

40. (2004). "Spreading Quality Education for the Deprived in Our Millennium: Latest Developments and a Proposal for South Asia". Paper presented at the *3rd Pan Commonwealth Conference on Open Learning*, and published in *the Proceedings,* held in July at Dunedin, New Zealand.

41. (2004). "Establishment of a Regional Open University for South Asia (ROUSA) in Dhaka." – *A Proposal submitted to SAARC Secretariat* by the present Author as the Convener, Study Group on the Proposed ROUSA. – University Alumni Forum of Bangladesh (Saudi Arabia Chapter), Riyadh. September.

42. (2000). "Academic Publishing and the University Presses: The Case in a Developing Region." *Journal of Scholarly Publishing.* (University of Toronto Press). Vol. 32, No. 1, pp 24-32. October.

43. (1994). "Scholarly Publishing in Developing Countries: The Role of Publishing Education Today for Development in the Next Century".

Paper presented at the 5th *International Conference on Scholarly Publishing*, 6-10 May. Aristotle University, Thessaloniki, Greece.

44. (1989). "Research and Scientific Publishing." *International Library Review*. London. Vol. 21, pp 355-361.

45. (1988). "Higher Education in Bangladesh: Open University as an Innovative Supplement to Resolving Some Problems". (in Bengali), In: *Bangladesher Mool Shomosya O' Taar Shomadhan* (*Major Issues in Bangladesh and Their Solutions*. UAFB, Riyadh. [Being the first ever article in Bengali on the open university concept].

46. From a forthcoming book on *Prokashona O' Shompadona Proshongo* (All About Publishing and Editing). Forthcoming, by a Bangladesh publisher from Dhaka

47. A Survey of Publications in Bengali in a Place Where the Language is Different. Survey conducted in Riyadh and published in the form of a Report. Dhaka University Alumni Forum, Saudi Arabia Chapter, Riyadh, 2004.

48. "Shushthu Shompadona O' Prokashona" (in Bengali) (Standard Editing and Publishing), Article published in the community magazine, *Mohona,* Bangladesh Writers' Forum, Riyadh. 2003.

49. Book: *Shikhyadan ebong Shikhyabaybostha* (Teaching and Educational Administration) written by Khaleda Manzur, and compiled, partly co-authored and edited by Manzurul Islam (two Articles on Education, Higher Education, also with some coverage to educational publishing and editing, etc.). 2002, 2011. The Scholar, Dhaka. 116 pp.

50. Book: *Shwadhinota, Muktijuddho, Probash Jibon O' Onnyannyo* (in Bengali) (Independendence, Liberation War, Expatriate Life and Other Essays); two Articles are on Higher Education, Open Learning, etc. (also slightly covering academic publishing, editing, quality assurance, etc.). 2002, 2011. The Scholar, Dhaka. 160 pp.

Forthcoming Publications:

1. (2016-). Editor-designate: *Bangladesh Journal of Open and Distance Learning* (bi-annual). [in preparation].
2. (2016). Editor / Compiler: *Capacity Building and Quality Assurance in Open and Distance Learning: Access to Higher Education by the Maximum Number of People* [in preparation].
3. (2016). Author / Editor: *Essays on Open and Distance Learning* [a collection of writings on the subject by the Author]
4. (2016). Author: *Towards a Regional Open and Virtual University for South and South East Asia: A Proposal. [Revised from the Author's earlier Proposals].*

9.2.2 **An Autobiographical Note about the Compiler / Author (MI) --- a publishing professional, an Academic and a Researcher --- and some documents related to Publishing and Editing, Quality Assurance, Open and Distance Learning (with indirect reference to the print media / publishing), etc.**

[An autobiographical note: In my rather long career spanning about five decades (1966 – 2015) with (i) teaching and research; (ii) publishing; (iii) training and education; (iv) communication via writing, editing and publishing; (v) open, virtual and distance learning, I preferred to maintain a low profile, like a quiet worker. Often I had to carry out some other responsibilities – social and personal (some requiring a higher profile). My engagements included some literary and journalistic pursuits too, not directly related to the above academic and professional ones.

Some details are provided here to inspire in some way or the other aspiring Bangladeshi publishing professionals, open and distance learning careerists, or academics with a checkered background].

Other works / studies on ODL (include):

– Have been involved in ODL ever since the first visit to Open Univ UK in 1973, and again during (1984 – 87) for a PhD from USA in 1987, on Education / Communication, via Distance and Open Learning.

- Attended the Workshop on Open University in Dhaka by Asian Development Bank and an Indian educational consultancy agency in 1991, little before the establishment of Bangladesh Open University (1992).

- Designed, developed and coordinated the one-week *Training Program on Capacity Building for ODL Materials* (12-19 March 2006), first of its kind in Bangladesh (for university Teachers,) and participated by 48 Associate Professors, Assistant Professors and Lecturers, mostly from Bangladesh Open University.

- Planned and directed the one-week *Training-cum-Workshop on Writing, Editing and Publishing*, for the ODL practitioners and officers, participated by 30 mid-level university executives (November, 2007) of Bangladesh Open University.

- Designed and directed a Workshop on ICT-based Education (Open and Virtual Learning) for University Courses, for academics and coordinators of Southeast University, Dhaka. (January, 2008).

- Designed and conducted a workshop on Editing and Publishing Academic Works, participated by officers of the University Grants Commission, Bangladesh. (March 2008).

- Have the distinction of being the first author in Bengali on Open University concept in Bangladesh through the publication of an article that appeared in 1988 in the book, *Bangladesher Mool Shomoshya O'Taar Somadhan.*: Unmukto Shikhyar Madhyome Uchcha Shikhya (Major Issues in Bangladesh and Their Solutions: Context / Higher Education through Open Learning). This was based on a Paper by the Author and presented by him in a Seminar in Riyadh in 1987. [Note: Bangladesh Open University was established in 1992.]

In addition to published materials as listed elsewhere (specially in Section 9.2.1), a few other **useful documents are available with the Author (MI):**

GENERAL: Worksheets or Handouts / Notes from Lectures / Courses attended or participated by the present Author / Compiler, specially at Oxford University (UK), Stanford University (USA), Simon Fraser University (Canada), and Open University of UK.

SPECIFIC:

- on Desktop Publishing (for the Education Sector), at Simon Fraser University, Vancouver, Canada, 1995;
- on Advance Publishing for Professionals, at Stanford University, California, USA, 1983;
- on Production, Design, Marketing and Rights sales / Copyrights, at different seminars, discussion sessions, and in international Book Fairs, specially in Karachi (1970), Frankfurt (1973, 1975, 1978), New Delhi (1976, 1979), Kolkata (several times), Belgrade (1978), Bahrain (1983), Cairo (1993), Thessaloniki, Greece (1994), New Zealand (2004), West Indies (2006), Cambridge (1973, 1984, 2007); London (at different times and again in 2008) ; and during different visits / discussions in the universities and university presses of Cambridge, Tokyo, Singapore, Hong Kong, Kuala Lumpur, Colombo, Kathmandu, Paris, The Hague, Toronto, Vancouver, Washington DC, New York, Boston (Harvard and MIT), and other academic and publishing places;
- on Advance Practices in Publishing Management at OUP, Oxford University, UK, 1973.
- Course Plan for a Masters Level program on Academic and Research Writing and Editing prepared by the present Author / Compiler, 1995 and revised in 2005 / 2012.

Currently also working in research, study and welfare and in development works on:

- Evaluation and quality assurance in ODL
- Training in Open Learning in Bangladesh
- Literacy programs for the rural adult (mostly women) through ODL / ICT initiatives
- Application of modern education (e.g. computer literacy, English, and Arithmetic) through ODL / ICT-enabled methods, for the youth in some selected rural and peri-urban areas of Bangladesh, and
- Programs related to education for all and higher education for the maximum number of people, through training of teachers and professionals in ODL and ICT-based activities (e.g. via English language development, etc).

Made study tours to several ODL and related institutions (during 1973, 1984, 1989, 1994, 1995-2002, 2004-2012) including:

: The Commonwealth of Learning, (COL), Vancouver, Canada
: Open Learning Agency of Canada, Vancouver; Canada
: Open University of UK, Milton Keynes, England
: International Extension College, Cambridge, England
: International Research Foundation for Open Learning (IRFOL), Cambridge, England
: External System, University of London, England
: Extension School, Harvard University, Cambridge, MA, USA
: Open Courseware Program, MIT, Cambridge, MA, USA
: Indira Gandhi National Open University, New Delhi, India
: Commonwealth Educational Media Center for Asia (CEMCA), New Delhi
: Arab Open University, Riyadh, Saudi Arabia
: Open University of Malaysia, Kuala Lumpur, and a few others.

Attended (and / or presented Papers in) some international conferences, including:

: UNED-ICDE 2013 International Conference on Open and Distance Education, held in Madrid, Spain, 7 – 9 March 2013) (could not attend, but submitted Paper accepted)
: The Fifth Pan Commonwealth Forum on ODL (held in London in 2008)
: The Fourth Pan Commonwealth Forum on ODL (held in Jamaica, West Indies in 2006)
: The Eleventh Cambridge International Conference on Open Learning (held in Cambridge, UK in 2005)
: The Third Pan Commonwealth Forum on ODL (held in Dunedin, New Zealand in 2004)

Carried out some promotional and advocacy works for open, distance and virtual learning in Bangladesh and the region through:

: Bangladesh Open University as its full-time Adviser, for 3 years (2005 – 2007).

: Southeast University, Dhaka as its full-time Adviser (and Director of its Center for Open and Virtual Learning, COViL), for 3 years (2008 – 2010).

: Center for Development through Open Learning, Publishing and Communication (CEDOLPC), Dhaka, as its Adjunct Chairman / Chief Consultant during 2007-2012, and now continuing as a full-timer since early – 2013.

: Bangladesh Society for Open, Virtual and Distance Learning (BASOVDiL), Dhaka, as its Honorary President since 2010.

: ZH Sikder University of Science & Technology (ZHSUST), Shariatpur, Bangladesh, as its founding Vice Chancellor (from early-May to December 2012) (having also planned for some proposed ICT-based ODL programs alongside traditional courses in this new, government-approved institution of higher education from a remote rural area).

: Commonwealth of Learning (COL), Vancouver, Canada. [being on its Roster of Consultants, since 2010].

: International Council for Open and Distance Learning (ICDE), Oslo, Norway. [being its Member since 2013].

Section 10

Index

[Acknowledgement: **Khaleda Manzur and Dulal Hossain, for their assistance in the preparation of the Index]**

234

Printed in the United States
By Bookmasters